Strange Snow

A Play in Two Acts

by Stephen Metcalfe

SAMUEL FRENCH, INC.

45 WEST 25TH STREET	NEW YORK 10010
7623 SUNSET BOULEVARD	HOLLYWOOD 90046
LONDON	*TORONTO*

"STRANGE SNOW" was commissioned by the **Manhattan Theatre Club** and received its world premiere there on January 19, 1982.

IMPORTANT ADVERTISING NOTE:

CREDIT AND BILLING REQUIREMENTS:

All advertisements and programs *must* give credit to the Author in all instances in which the title of the Play appears. Billing of the Author shall appear immediately following the title, on a separate line on which no other name appears, and shall be in a size of type at least 50% the size of the Title type.

In addition: the following announcement *must* appear on the first page of credits in all programs:
"STRANGE SNOW" was commissioned by the MANHATTAN THEATRE CLUB and received its world premiere there on January 20, 1982.

Manhattan Theatre Club

UpStage

Artistic Director
LYNNE MEADOW

Managing Director
BARRY GROVE

presents

STRANGE SNOW

by

STEVE METCALFE

with

CHRISTOPHER CURRY   DANN FLOREK
KAIULANI LEE

Set Design
ATKIN PACE

Costume Designer
NAN CIBULA

Lighting Design
CHERYL THACKER

Production Stage Manager
LORETTA ROBERTSON

Directed by
THOMAS BULLARD

January 19- February 21, 1982

Associate Artistic Director
DOUGLAS HUGHES

General Manager
CONNIE L. ALEXIS

MTC productions are made possible in part with public funds from the National Endowment for the Arts and the New York State Council on the Arts.

*   *   *

STRANGE SNOW was specially commissioned by the Manhattan Theatre Club with the aid of public funds from the National Endowment for the Arts.

5

CAST
(in order of appearance)

Megs .... Dann Florek
Martha .... Kaiulani Lee
David .... Christopher Curry

The action of the play takes place within a twenty-four hour period in the Flanagan home.

Time: the present

There will be one ten-minute intermission.

Production Staff for
STRANGE SNOW

Production Stage Manager .... Loretta Robertson
Stage Manager .... Mari S. Schatz
Assistant to Ms. Thacker .... Rich Buffington
Electrician .... Janine Gittens
Production Intern .... Amy Sicular

Casting .... DEBORAH BROWN
Casting Assistants .... Maryellen Mulcahy
Eva Saks

Merchandising .... Ruth Sussman Associates
Make-up Consultant .... Peg Schierholz

Strange Snow

ACT ONE

SCENE 1

(*The lights come up on MEGS on the porch, stage left. HE looks in the window for signs of life. Nothing. HE begins banging on the front door.*)

MEGS. Rise and shine, you sweet bear! It's time! The fishy-wishies are waitin for us like whores in heat! We're the drunkest sailors on the block! Hah!? Hah!? (*Nothing. HE comes off the porch, looks upstairs.*) Wake up, you great fool! We're gonna dance on Charlie the Tuna's grave! (*HE does a quick dance. Waits. Nothing. HE comes onto the porch again. HE bangs on the door.*) Davey!? You up or what, guy? Hello? Rise and shine! Bed is for lovers or invalids, huh! Davey! Yo, Davey! You awake!?

(*A light comes on in the stairwell. MARTHA comes roaring down the stairs. SHE is carrying a golf club. SHE is in robe and slippers. SHE wears glasses.*)

MARTHA. Stop it! Stop that noise! Stop it! (*SHE glares at MEGS through the panes of glass in the door. SHE brandishes the golf club threateningly.*) If I have to come out there, you'll be sorry. I know how to use this! (*HE stops banging. HE grins.*)

7

MEGS. Well, hi there, little lady. Nice mornin, huh? Kinda cold for golf though. Dark too. You always go golfin in your p.j.'s? You got mud cleats in your slippers? (*SHE glares at HIM, turns, puts down the club, goes to the phone.*) Who you callin? You're gonna wake'm up.

MARTHA. I'm calling the police.

MEGS. Why you callin the police, woman?

MARTHA. I suggest you run. The police will come and they'll arrest you.

MEGS. Why would they want to do that?

MARTHA. Hello? Yes, I'd like the police. (*for MEGS' benefit*) I'd like to report a disturbance.

MEGS. Hey, come on, I'm no disturbance. I'm a friend a Davey's!

MARTHA. David?

MEGS. Dave Flanagan. This is his place, ain't it?

MARTHA. David is in bed. At this hour most people are! You'd better have a very good reason for making such a racquet.

MEGS. (*grinning*) I wake you?

MARTHA. (*crosses left*) Of course you woke me! You scared me to death!

MEGS. I'm a buddy a Davey's.

MARTHA. I've never seen you here before.

MEGS. I've never been invited. But I'm a friend. Honest. (*pause*)

MARTHA. (*crosses right center*) Yes, hello? Could you please send a squad car to—

MEGS. No, wait, listen! You must be Davey's sister, Martha! (*pause*)

MARTHA. I don't know you!

MEGS. I feel like I know you! Davey talked about you all the time. Said you're swell. (*pause*)

MARTHA. Nevermind. (*SHE hangs up the phone. Moves to the door, unlocks it, opens it a crack. MEGS sticks his head in, grins.*)

MEGS. Joseph Megessey. Everybody calls me Megs. (*MARTHA frowns at HIM as if there is a bud taste in her mouth.*)

MARTHA. Megs.

MEGS. That's my name, don't wear it out.

MARTHA. It's a ridiculous name.

MEGS. Ain't it? (*pause*) Your brother and me, see, we're goin fishin.

MARTHA. Fishing.

MEGS. Yeah. It's opening day!

MARTHA. Ridiculous. The sun's not even up.

MEGS. Exactly. See, those trout'll be so bleary eyed, they'll think our nightcrawlers are filet mignon. They'll go for em. Pow! And you know what we'll do, Martha? We'll bring'm home here and cook'm up for your dinner. What a you think a that? (*SHE retreats from the door, crosses left, letting HIM in. MEGS enters.*)

MARTHA. I think you're a fool. (*SHE turns on lights in the living room.*)

MEGS. (*following*) No-o! It's opening day! The luck is rolling off me in waves! Smell? Perfume, huh? (*MEGS crosses to MARTHA.*)

MARTHA. Don't come near me. You smell like dirt.

MEGS. No! Nightcrawlers! (*HE displays a plastic baggy filled with nightcrawlers.*) Hey, Martha! You want to come?

MARTHA. What? Where?

MEGS. Fishin! I bet there's a rainbow that long just waitin with your name on it. M-A-R-T-H-A!

MARTHA. Ridiculous.

MEGS. No! Listen, what say you go on upstairs and

give your brother a poke in the breadbasket. Get him on down here.

MARTHA. (*crosses to door, closing it, brushing past HIM to close the door that HE has left wide open*) I will not! I'll have you know I was up till two in the morning correcting papers!

MEGS. Hey, no you weren't! On a Friday night?

MARTHA. Every night!

MEGS. I bet you was out hullaballooin under the moon. I bet you got home five minutes ago and you threw on that robe to fool me!

MARTHA. You're preposterous.

MEGS. Ya can't fool me woman! You got moonburns on your cheeks like roses!

MARTHA. I do not!

MEGS. Do!

MARTHA. Be quiet! (*MARTHA crosses to door. SHE tries to move past HIM and HE sweeps HER into his arms.*)

MEGS. Opening day, Martha! (*And HE dances HER around the furniture. Dances MARTHA up left to up right, then up center, and finally twirls MARTHA into chair, ending up on top of HER.*)

MEGS. Grab your partner. Dance your partner, swing your partner!	MARTHA. How dare you! Stop! You can't just . . . I'm not dressed for—stop!

MEGS. Skip to the lue, my darlin! (*And HE deposits HER in a chair.*) Thank you, mam! Ginger Rogers and Fred Astaire better look out, huh? Yeah . . . Uh, you think Davey's up? (*crosses left to end of couch*)

MARTHA. (*crosses down stage left of chair*) Joseph, I don't think David remembered he made a date to go fishing with you.

MEGS. Opening day?

MARTHA. He wasn't home when I went to bed at two.

MEGS. Naw, he musta remembered. (*crosses up right to stairs, yelling up the stairs*) C'mon guy! I got my waders in the car! God, it's good to meet you, Martha. (*Crosses down to stage left of MARTHA. HE shakes her hand.*) Davey, he talked about you all the time, said you're swell. Hey, has he ever mentioned me to you?

MARTHA. I'd of remembered if if he had.

MEGS. (*grinning*) Yeah. (*SHE yawns.*) Would you look at me keeping you up? You oughta be in dreamland restin up for good ol Saturday night. Don't worry about me. I'm fine. I'll sit right here and wait. (*crosses to stage right end of sofa*) Go. Go to bed. (*HE sits. HE "waits". pause*)

MARTHA. I'll tell him you're here. He won't like it. (*crosses upstage, pause*) He hates being woken up. (*pause, SHE starts to leave, crosses upstairs, SHE stops*) He throws alarm clocks through windows. (*No response. SHE goes upstairs. Pause. SHE comes back down and proceeds briskly to the door with the intention of asking HIM to leave*) I'm not going to do it. He'll take it out on me the rest of the day. (*There is the sound of a toilet flushing from upstairs.*)

MEGS. Somebody's up! (*crosses up right to foot of stairs*) I hear something flushing down the drain. Let's hope it's not last night's dinner. (*calling up the stairs*) Bout time, dude! Let's get a move on! I'm borin your poor sister to death!

MARTHA. (*crosses to kitchen; puts club down behind

trash can, turns to sink; MEGS follows, stands stage right of HER) Why don't I get coffee on. You'll probably both need it.

MEGS. Hey, I'm fine.

MARTHA. Let me put it this way. David is going to need it.

MEGS. Don't go to any trouble.

MARTHA. I assure you, I won't. I'm up. (*with a touch of sarcasm*) I'm an early riser. (*and THEY move into the kitchen*)

MEGS. (*MARTHA fills kettle, puts it on stove*) Know something? Me too. Up with the milk man every day. Listen, you do coffee and then Davey and I'll go. I got food and drink in the car. I planned ahead. We are gonna eat better'n turkeys on the first a November. Osmosis, see. The trout are gonna feel it in the air that we're fat and happy and they're gonna be so jealous they'll (*MARTHA puts coffee in pot.*) be chompin on air bubbles. Hey! Look at this! (*HE takes what appears to be a large, brightly colored dustball from his pocket. HE places it ceremoniously on the table.*)

MARTHA. What is it?

MEGS. It's a fly. I tied it myself. Ya like it?

MARTHA. It's colorful.

MEGS. Oh, goddam, it is that, ain't it. I figure it'll either drive a fish mad with passion or scare'm half to death. Lotta hair and all of it cowlicks. Sorta like you, woman.

MARTHA. (*Her hands go to hair.*) What? Oh . . . it's a mess, isn't it.

MEGS. Oh, no, Martha. It's fine. It's just fine . . . uh, I wonder what's keepin that big guy. Think I oughta go bounce on his belly? (*MEGS crosses to living room, crosses back through doorway.*)

MARTHA. I don't think that would be a wise idea. Joseph . . . there are beer cans in the wastebasket. They're David's discards. From last night. Before he went out.(*HE nudges the wastebasket. Cans rattle.*)

MEGS. From last night? Oh. He forgot, didn't he.

MARTHA. I'm afraid so.

MEGS. Yeah. Well . . . it's o.k. My fault. My dumb mistake. (*MEGS gets fly, crosses to living room.*)

MARTHA. Joseph —

MEGS. No! Davey's a busy guy, drivin those trucks here and there and back again. Who has time for fishin. Hey, it's been real good to meet you, Martha. I'm sorry I woke you. I'll let myself out. (*Crosses downstage of couch to door. HE begins to exit. Pause.*)

MARTHA. (*Crosses to living room. Crosses to foot of stairs.*) Joseph? This is ridiculous but . . . he's had hangovers before . . . DAVID!? DAVID! GET UP THIS MINUTE! YOU'RE GOING FISHING!

MEGS. You think he heard?

MARTHA. I'm sure the whole neighborhood did. DAVID!

MEGS. (*crosses to stage right of MARTHA*) GET YOUR BUTT IN GEAR, GUY! PULL ON YOUR DRAWERS AND PUT SOME DOUBLE KNOTS IN YOUR SNEAKERS! WE GOTTA CATCH A TROUT FOR MARTHA'S DINNER!

MARTHA. YOU'VE GOT TO CATCH A TROUT FOR MY DINNER!

MEGS. You like trout, do ya?

MARTHA. I've never had them.

MEGS. Well, I've never caught'm but there's a first time for everything.

MARTHA. (*crosses downstage of chair*) I bet there's a recipe in one of my cookbooks.

MEGS. (*crosses stage right of MARTHA*) You fry'm!
You dump'm in corn flour and then whip'm into bacon
grease and they come out brown and tasty.

MARTHA. If you catch them and *clean* them, I'll cook
them.

MEGS. You will? You're on, Martha. There's one sit-
tin under a log waitin for us and know what? It has your
name right across the rainbow. M-A-R-T-H-A!! (*And
HE sweeps HER into his arms again. THEY dance
down stage left.*)

MEGS. Swing your part- ner. Glide your partner round and round. Skip to to the lue, my darlin!	MARTHA. Joseph, put me down . . . you can't just . . . oh!

(*And MARTHA breaks into helpless giggles. DAVE
enters down to the bottom of the stairs. HE is in
boxer shorts and is horribly hung over. MARTHA
and MEGS stop at the sight of HIM.*)

DAVE. What in hell is goin on?

MEGS. (*crosses upstage of couch, HE grins, pause*)
You're up! (*pause*) Look at you! Wouldn't go off a high
dive in those johns, guy!

DAVE. What do you two think you're doing?

MARTHA. You and Joseph are going fishing, David.

DAVE. You're out of your mind.

MEGS. It's opening day, guy.

DAVE. Raincheck. (*Crosses to kitchen fridge. MEGS
crosses to sink.*)

MARTHA. David, you made a date to go fishing.
Joseph has the car loaded and ready to go.

DAVE. Joseph?

MEGS. I got beer, sandwiches. It's a great adventure, guy.

DAVE. We plan this? (*MARTHA crosses to doorway.*)

MEGS. Hey, last week. McDonalds, remember? How you been, I said. Good, you said. We oughta get together, said me. Fine, said you. Fishing said me, opening day. Opening day, said you. Hah?! Hah!? Guess what today is, guy!!

DAVE. I thought fishing season was in the fall.

MEGS. No, that's huntin. Don't worry, we'll do that too when the time comes. Opening day, Davey!

DAVE. I can't. (*Crosses to living room, to couch; MEGS follows*)

MEGS. Opening day?

DAVE. Sorry.

MEGS. Rainbows this long.

DAVE. Not up to it.

MEGS. Sure you are, Davey. A big ol nightcrawler on a hook? That'll perk your ass up. I got one here so big those rainbows'll have to be careful he don't eat them. (*And HE proudly displays one to DAVEY who almost gets sick.*)

DAVE. Yech.

MARTHA. Go take a shower. You'll feel better.

DAVE. I'm passing.

MARTHA. You're doing no such thing. Shower and get dressed. I'll make breakfast for you both.

DAVE. I don't want to do fishing, Martha.

MARTHA. You're going.

DAVE. I don't want to go fishing.

MARTHA. David, I want a trout. Fried in corn flour. There's one waiting with my name on it.

MEGS. Davey? Hey, Davey? C'mon, guy. It'll be a great time. There's frost in the air and wondrous strange snow on the ground. The trout streams are gurglin and singing. Know what they're sayin? Wake up, Davey. It's time. It's time. Openin day with your ol buddy, Megs. Damn! Makes me want to paint my face and pretend I'm Hiawatha. Whoo-whoo-whoo-whoo! *Fish*-ing! *Fish*-ing! (*MEGS war dances down left. HE keeps up his noise till DAVE says O.K.*)

DAVE. Megs, I . . . I don't . . . ahh! O.K.!! (*exiting*) I must have a screw loose.

MEGS. Never doubted it for a minute.

DAVE. I'm sleeping in the car.

MEGS. (*MEGS crosses to foot of stairs.*) You'll sleep, I'll drive. Hey! You're beautiful! Don't you ever forget that.

DAVE. (*off-stage*) God.

MARTHA. He didn't look very beautiful to me. Not in those baggy drawers of his.

MEGS. (*MEGS crosses center stage left of MARTHA.*) Martha, you're too much, you know that? You are. Something. He was not gonna go and you talked him into it.

MARTHA. I didn't talk him into anything.

MEGS. (*putting his hands affectionately on her arms*) Ain't you modest, I saw.

MARTHA. (*coldly*) I was making coffee. (*Crosses to kitchen. And SHE enters the kitchen. HE follows.*)

MEGS. Hey, y'know, Martha, instant's fine with me. I drink so much instant my stomach's freeze dried.

MARTHA. I find instant coffee foul. You'll have to make do with ground for drip. (*SHE pours water in coffee pot. MEGS crosses to stage right of MARTHA.*)

MEGS. Drip? We'll go for it! I'll pretend I fell asleep and woke up in Dunkin Donuts. Hey, you got any milk? (*And HE sticks his nose in the refrigerator.*)

MARTHA. (*annoyed*) Yes, of course I've got milk.

MEGS. (*bringing it out*) Thank god for that. Powdered creamer? (*puts milk on counter, HE sits on counter*) I hate that shit. It tastes like powered mouseballs to me. (*pause*) Oh goddam, listen to me talk. (*MEGS gets off counter.*) Give me a bar a soap and I'll wash my mouth out as far down as my tonsils. Maybe it'll learn me to talk like a human being in front of a lady.

MARTHA. (*MARTHA puts cream and sugar on table.*) A lady? Really . . . Besides, I'm used to it. I teach high school students, mouthes like spittoons.

MEGS. Rap'm smartly upside the head. That'll learn'm.

MARTHA. (*MARTHA puts mugs on table.*) My major was in biology, not the martial arts.

MEGS. Well, you ever have any problems, you let me know. I'm not good for much but one thing I could do is put the fear a god into a bunch a (*MARTHA gets spoons, puts them on table.*) young punks. They oughta be bringin you apples and candy and havin crushes on you and stuff.

MARTHA. That'll be the day. (*pause*) You must have been a delightful student. (*MARTHA crosses to fridge, gets orange juice.*)

MEGS. Me? Oh no, I was never any good at school. I specialized in phys-ed, auto shop and smokin in the lavatories. I'da driven you crazy. (*MEGS sits in chair, stage right.*)

MARTHA. I doubt it. I've developed a high tolerance level.

MEGS. I woulda. I could never keep my mouth shut. Everybody'd be laughin. Not with me, at me. I didn't care. I liked the attention. (*Pause. MARTHA puts juice on table.*) Hey, you, Martha! I bet you was a hell of a student. (*Pause. SHE looks at HIM suspiciously.*) Well, were ya?

MARTHA. Yes, I was. I was mad for it.

MEGS. No!

MARTHA. (*proudly*) I loved to study. Straight A's in every subject.

MEGS. You're something, Martha. It must be great to be so smart.

MARTHA. (*gloating*) Yes, it is.

MEGS. (*MARTHA pours milk into creamer, crosses to table.*) I was dumber'n paint. But I sure as hell woulda brought you apples and candy, Martha. You can bet your sweet ass on that! (*And without thinking HE swats HER on the rump.*)

MEGS. Sorry.

MARTHA. What would you like for breakfast? (*crosses to fridge*)

MEGS. Hey, anything. Everything. My eyes could be bigger'n basketballs, they still wouldn't be bigger'n my stomach.

MARTHA. I like pancakes on Saturday mornings.

MEGS. I do too. I love'm. Give me pancakes and the roadrunner on t.v. and Saturday morning is complete.

MARTHA. I like sausage too.

MEGS. Squealers!? Sausage goes good with pancakes.

MARTHA. You'll have that then?

MEGS. Sausage and pancakes?

MARTHA. Would you rather eggs?

MEGS. Hey, how bout all three?

MARTHA. Why didn't I think of that. (*gets flour from top of fridge*)

MEGS. Goddam, Martha! Eggs and pancakes and sausage, it feels like Easter or something. (*MEGS drinks juice. MARTHA crosses to sink; gets skillet under-neath.*) And do you know what we'll have to go with it? Beer! I got a couple a cases in the car.

MARTHA. For breakfast? That's horrible.

MEGS. Breakfast beer. It's the best kind. Martha, ain't you ever had a beer for breakfast?

MARTHA. Joseph, there are those of us who have never had a beer.

MEGS. No! Woman, you are in for a treat. You sip on a breakfast beer and first thing you know, the cobwebs go, your voice rises two octaves, and god almighty, the sun comes up inside you! I'll go get some! (*And HE runs out of the kitchen, through the living room and out the front door.*)

MARTHA. Joseph, I hardly . . . all right. (*SHE begins to take things from the refrigerator. DAVE, dressed, comes down the stairs and into the kitchen. HE looks around.*)

DAVE. He leave?

MARTHA. He went to the car to get beer.

DAVE. (*DAVE crosses to chair center, sits.*) Good. I could use one.

MARTHA. David, it happens to be five in the morning.

DAVE. You better believe it.

MARTHA. The idea is nauseating. You can't drink beer.

DAVE. I can. What an asshole.

MARTHA. Sshh. He'll hear you.

DAVE. I was talking about me. I wish you hadn't sided with him, Martha. He was gonna leave.

MARTHA. He looked so hurt when he thought you might have forgotten.

DAVE. I had forgotten. Martha, why is it you're a

hardass with everything but stray animals? Bring'm in, give'm a warm bowl of milk, who ends up cleaning the turds off the floor? Me.

MARTHA. (*SHE pours HIM coffee.*) Hardly. Besides, your friend doesn't qualify as an animal.

DAVE. (*preoccupied*) He's not my friend. He's just somebody I know. We were in Viet Nam together.

MARTHA. (*interested*) Oh. (*pause*) I like him.

DAVE. You don't know him, sis.

MARTHA. I'm entitled to my first impressions. (*returns pot to stove*) He's endearing is what he is.

DAVE. Endearing? (*HE laughs.*) God, Martha, what do you know about endearing. (*HE sips from the coffee she has brought HIM. HE makes a face. MARTHA crosses to chair stage right, drinks juice.*) I wish he'd hurry up with that beer.

MARTHA. I wouldn't think you could stomach it after all you had last night. I assume the empties were just the start.

DAVE. Come on. I work hard all week. I'm entitled to cut lose on the weekend. You ought to try it sometime. It'd do you good. (*pause*)

MARTHA. I'd love to. You can take me with you tonight.

DAVE. (*again preoccupied*) Forget it.

MARTHA. Why not? All you ever do is go out with the boys. I'd think you might like a woman around for a change.

DAVE. Women we can use, a sister we don't need. Besides, I date.

MARTHA. I've seen the kind of woman you date. Their idea of contributing to a conversation is to snap their chewing gum. Don't you think you might like a point of view for a change?

DAVE. I want a point of view, I'll listen to the news.

MARTHA. I'll be silent then. Unresponsive, unob-
trusive, the kind of women men like.

DAVE. How do you know what men like? (*laughing*)
God, Martha, you're too much, you know that? You've
hardly been out with anybody in your whole life but
you're the authority on the suject.

MARTHA. David? Piss up a rope. (*MARTHA crosses
up right to counter.*)

DAVE. (*surprised*) What I'd say already?

MARTHA. Just . . . drink your juice.

(*MEGS rushes through the front door, through the
living room and into the kitchen. HE is carrying
two sixes of beer. HE puts them on the counter.*)

MEGS. Beer! We got it! I had to chop it out of the ice
chest with a screwdriver! Be careful, it's colder than
Alaska. One for you, one for me, and the by-god coldest
of the bunch for you, Martha. Blow on it first, otherwise your tongue'll stick to the can. (*HE holds out a
beer to MARTHA.*)

DAVE. Forget it, Megs. Martha doesn't drink beer.

MEGS. Oh. Well, hey, it is early. (*And HE flips it in
the air, catches it and sets it down.*)

DAVE. Any time of the day is too early for her.

MARTHA. David? (*And MARTHA picks up the can of
beer.*)

DAVE. Yeah?

MARTHA. To opening day. (*SHE opens it. Shaken, it
sprays HER. Undaunted SHE takes a mammouth gulp.*)

MEGS. To opening day, by damn! (*SHE takes the can
down from her lips. Her eyes are watering and SHE is
breathless.*)

DAVE. (*sarcastic*) How's it taste, sis?

MARTHA. (*raising the can in toast*) To trout! (*SHE takes an even bigger gulp.*)

MEGS. (*impressed*) Are we gonna catch us the limit or what! Breakfast beer, Martha! (*Pause as MARTHA struggles to hold it down.*)

MARTHA. (*breathless but with a challenging look at DAVID*) I have a confession, Joseph. I think I like beer.

DAVE. Terrific.

MEGS. I should say so! Finish that one off, I'll crack you another one. (*hands MARTHA another can*)

MARTHA. I'll take it upstairs. (*crosses to kitchen doorway*) I'll have to get dressed if I'm coming with you.

DAVE. What?

MEGS. You're coming along, Martha?

MARTHA. You invited me.

MEGS. Oh, this is so great. The rainbows'll never know what hit'm.

MARTHA. (*crosses to up right of DAVE, slapping DAVE on the shoulder*) Yes, I'm sure they'll be jumping in my lap dying to hear my women's point of view. (*SHE starts to exit stage right.*)

DAVE. Forget it, Martha.

MARTHA. Joseph doesn't mind, do you, Joseph?

MEGS. Mind? I should say not. I'm happy you're coming, Martha. If I'da known you wanted to, I'da asked you twice.

MARTHA. (*exiting*) I'll get ready. (*MARTHA crosses up center—upstairs. MEGS crosses up center to bottom of stair.*)

MEGS. And don't you worry about breakfast. We'll stop along the way is what we'll do. We'll eat enough pancakes to build a house. On me! A woman doesn't buy when I'm around.

DAVE. (*sarcastic*) Dress warm, sis.

MARTHA. (*offstage*) David!?

DAVE. Yeah?

MARTHA. Up a rope!

MEGS. (*laughing, crosses to kitchen up left of DAVE*) She's great, your sister, I like her. (*HE puts on a Boston Red Sox hat that HE pulls from his pocket. It is old and well worn.*) Hah!? Hah!? Opening day and we're goin for it. (*crosses stage right of DAVE*)

DAVE. Let's not.

MEGS. Huh?

DAVE. Let's say we have Martha make us some breakfast, we'll shoot the shit awhile, and you hit the road and let me get some sleep cause let me tell you, Megs, I don't feel good.

MEGS. (*MEGS sits in chair, stage right.*) You didn't recognize the hat, did ya. I wear it for luck.

DAVE. Bad luck, huh?

MEGS. It's changed it's ways. It didn't like it over there in Nam any better than we did. It's not mine, it's Bobby's.

DAVE. Didn't help ol Bobby much, did it?

MEGS. It's helpin me.

DAVE. Listen, don't get started.

MEGS. Sorry. (*pause*)

DAVE. So . . . don't see around much, Megs.

MEGS. I been puttin a lot of hours at the garage. Hey, sweet bear, I opened up my own garage.

DAVE. You quit drivin?

MEGS. It was time. Time to give those whores a rest, huh?

DAVE. Tell me about it.

MEGS. Yeah, but you're still barrelassin cross them amber waves a grain, aint'cha.

DAVE. Got a cake run. Produce distribution. Suits me fine.

MEGS. You ride'm, I'll repair'm! Did you know they hide under rocks?

DAVE. Who?

MEGS. Trout, guy! The speckled little bastards, they hide under rocks! Now what kind of a life is that, huh?

DAVE. You ever caught a trout?

MEGS. (*sheepish*) No . . . but I been practicin! I been casting in the backyard! I had that line singing through the air like a bullwhip! Till I got snagged. Neighbor's sheet. Ripped the hell out it. Boy, was she pissed. Good fishermen file the barbs off their hooks.

DAVE. Come on. Who told you that?

MEGS. T.V.! The American Sportsman! Watch Don Meredith hunt anacondas with a bowie knife! Trout fishin! You file off the barbs so they have a chance.

DAVE. Right. We gonna do that?

MEGS. No fuckin way, Jose!! Don't tell, Martha, stud, but I got a feelin the only way I'm gonna catch a fish is to drain the pond. We'll see! We'll see! Damn! This trout fishin is a good time!

DAVE. Great. Terrific.

MEGS. Y'know, I only wear Bobby's hat on special occasions.

DAVE. Megs—

MEGS. No, really! Like when one of my kids needs a homerun. (*stands up right a few steps*)

DAVE. Kids? What kids?

MEGS. Hey, I coached little league this last summer. Pee-wees. We screamed and hollered and lost every game. They want me for this year too. They like me.

DAVE. You're just a likable guy. God . . . I gotta lie down. (*DAVE enters the living room. HE lies on the couch. MEGS follows.*)

MEGS. (*MEGS crosses to up center of couch.*) A home run in the ninth!?

DAVE. What?

MEGS. You liked the Yankees, Bobby liked the Red Soxs. You guys bet. Bobby won on Carl Yastrzemski's homerun in the ninth.

DAVE. That's right. Five bucks we bet.

MEGS. He loved those Red Soxs, huh? Ol Bobby? Crazy for'm. He wanted us all to go to Fenway Park, remember? Beer and hotdogs, huh? Scream till we're hoarse. We oughta do that sometime, sweet Davey. Baseball season's just around the corner.

DAVE. Forget it.

MEGS. It'd be fun.

DAVE. Forget it.

MEGS. How come?

DAVE. (*pause*) Hold out your hands.

MEGS. (*MEGS up right a few steps, hiding them*) Aw, Davey . . . I ain't put my fists through glass in a long time.

DAVE. I've heard that before.

MEGS. Look at me now, Davey, huh? Look at me. Fat and happy. I bet you never seen me looking so good, guy.

DAVE. You look the same as before. (*sarcastic*) Guy.

MEGS. (*With an edge, crosses to stage left of couch.*) And you. You look real good too. And you just *stagger* into me in the parking lot of ol McDonald land. Damn. Fate's a funny thing. (*pause*) So talk to me some, huh?

DAVE. Talk? About what? (*And DAVE rises, goes to the liquor cabinet, gets a bottle of whiskey from underneath. HE takes a sip, offers it to MEGS.*)

MEGS. Never touch it, stud. Be wasted on me. Be like puttin ethyl alcohol in a lawnmower. (*MEGS is at the trophy case. HE picks up a photo.*)

MEGS. These your folks, huh?

DAVE. Huh? Yeah.

MEGS. Nice lookin Mom. Sorta like Martha.

DAVE. She moved to Florida about a year ago. She didn't like the cold. She calls once a week and she and Martha gang up on me.

MEGS. Maybe too many memories of your Dad around here too, huh?

DAVE. Maybe.

MEGS. Musta been tough, Davey. Musta been real tough. You come hobblin off the plane on those crutches a yours and they lay that on you.

DAVE. Yeah. I was pissed. It was my Dad's gung-ho vet shit that got me to enlist in the first place and I'd been fantasizing for months on how the first thing I was gonna do was deck the son of a bitch. I felt cheated.

MEGS. (*picking up a photograph*) Hey, is this Martha? (*Dave looks, laughs*) Whoo, she's changed, stud. Blossomed. (*picking up a plaque*) And would you look at this? All league!

DAVE. Team captain.

MEGS. (*picking up another photo*) Goddam! Look at you! Nice tie, studhoss. When's this?

DAVE. Senior year.

MEGS. Would ya look at them apple cheeks?

DAVE. Future fuckin lawyers club.

MEGS. You was gonna be a lawyer, Davey?

DAVE. What?

MEGS. You know, was that what you was, like, plannin? To be a lawyer? After?

DAVE. I was gonna be everything, man. You name it, I was gonna be it.

MEGS. Hey. Know what all this is, Davey? Memories. Stuff to show your kids.

DAVE. Come off it, man. It's a bad joke. Something

out of Archie Comics. (*crosses to bottom of stairs*) Hey,
Martha! Let's go if we're going to go!

MEGS. (*crosses to stage left of DAVE*) Dress warm,
woman! We want you to catch rainbows, not your death
a cold! Hey, sweet Davey, you think maybe she likes
me?

DAVE. (*crosses to down left window*) Come off it,
man. You two are from different planets. Only reason
she's comin along is to bust my ass.

MEGS. Oh. Yeah. I guess you're right. (*pause*)

MEGS. (*MEGS crosses to down left window, stands up
right of DAVE.*) Sun's coming up. Real pretty. Remember
the sunrises? Over there? They were beauties, huh?
Yeah. Remember what old Bobby'd say? If it wasn't for
the C-rations we could pretend we was in Hawaii.
Remember him sayin that? I do. (*pause*) Know what I
hated? The waiting.

DAVE. Yeah. They always had to let us know in ad-
vance when we'd be goin out.

MEGS. Me, I never got used to it. Made me want to
piss my pants every time. Only way I could bear it was
to get up for it, y'know? Something set in. It was like I
was numb and speedin at the same time.

DAVE. Christ, you listening to yourself?

MEGS. Just talkin.

DAVE. What you're talking about! We're not there,
we're here!

MEGS. Damn right! We're here and now and that's
what counts. Talking doesn't hurt, Davey. (*pause*)
Maybe you don't do it often enough.

DAVE. (*crosses stage right*) I was never there, Megs.

MEGS. I ain't followin that.

DAVE. (*crosses to MEGS*) Look, as far as I'm con-
cerned it never happened. It's done with, understand?

MEGS. How come I'm standin here then?

DAVE. You got me.

MEGS. How come I'm wearin Bobby's lucky hat?

DAVE. Burn the fuckin thing.

MEGS. It was Bobby's.

DAVE. Bury it with him. (*And HE suddenly knocks the hat from MEG's head. An ugly silence.*)

DAVE. Yeah . . . this trout fishing is a great time. (*MEGS picks up the hat. Pause. HE begins picking up empty beer cans. MEGS gets cans from shelf; from magazine rack.*) Hey, listen . . . Megs . . . leave that stuff. Martha'll do it.

MEGS. My pleasure, stud. (*AND MARTHA comes down the stairs.*) By god, woman, look at you! Straight out of an L.L. Bean Catalogue!! The fish are gonna take one look at you and walk out of the water with their hands up!

MARTHA. Thank you.

DAVE. Better get your glasses on or you'll trip over them when they do.

MARTHA. I don't need them. I have on contact lenses.

DAVE. Contacts!?

MARTHA. I've had them. I'll take those, Joseph. (*crosses to MEGS, takes cans, turns towards kitchen*) They get under foot like marbles, don't they? (*And a hard look passes between DAVE and MARTHA.*)

DAVE. Have another beer, sis. Where'd you get the clothes.

MARTHA. I took some of my classes on a field trip to a fresh water pond. I couldn't very well collect samples in a skirt.

MEGS. Hell, no. Would I change a muffler in a three piece suit? You look terrific, Martha, just terrific. God, are we going to catch the limit or what? Listen, I'll start the car. Opening day, (*HE takes out fly; waves it.*) ladies and gentlemen, opening day! Look out, trout, we're on our way! (*HE grabs the beer and exits. Exit up left. Pause.*)

MARTHA. You're drinking.

DAVE. You want to try this too?

MARTHA. I'll pass, thank you. You ready?

DAVE. Who you trying to impress, Martha, huh? Contact lenses? You drinking beer? Give me a break.

MARTHA. What is wrong, David, with me having a good time for once?

DAVE. (*gesturing in MEGS direction*) You're that desperate?

MARTHA. He's nice.

DAVE. Or maybe he's just as desperate as you.

MARTHA. (*softly*) Fuck you, David.

DAVE. Ooh, Miss Peach! Nice mouth for a school teacher. You talk that way to your students?

MARTHA. No. (*pause*) Go back to bed if you want to. I'm going fishing. (*SHE exits.*)

DAVE. (*crosses toward door*) Go on. The two of you have a great time! Hell with you both! (*Crosses to couch. Pause. There is the sound of a car starting up, revving. DAVE runs to the door.*) Martha!? I'm coming! (*HE grabs his jacket, a fatigue jacket. HE picks up the bottle. HE exits.*) I wouldn't miss this for the world.

LIGHTS TO BLACK

ACT ONE

SCENE 2

(*MARTHA enters through the kitchen door, stage right. SHE has a blanket around HER. Her pants and shoes are wet. Her hair is damp. SHE is shivering with cold.*)

MARTHA. Ohh . . . (*SHE runs through the kitchen, into the living room and runs up the stairs. Pause.*)

MEGS. Martha! Hey, Martha!? (*MEGS enters through the kitchen door. DAVEY is out cold over his shoulder. DAVE groans.*) It's a-o.k., sweet bear. I gotcha. My wits are weak but my back is strong. (*HE almost slips.*) Whoops! Good christ, guy, there's water on the floor. I almost took us both out. (*DAVE groans.*) You gonna be sick again? You alive back there, hah? Hey, nobody ever said trout fishing was gonna be easy. Martha!!? (*HE enters the living room. Crosses to center left.*) Whew, you are heavy, stud. We'll have to make room for you in the trophy case. Have you stuffed and we'll hang a little sign on you. This is what we brought back alive. Barely. Martha, where'd you go, woman!? Don't worry, stud, we'll follow the puddles, we'll find her. Let's get you settled, stud. (*HE puts DAVE on the couch.*) It's o.k., sweet bear, it's a-o.k. Some of us, we didn't drink, we'd cut our wrists, huh? You don't have to explain. I know. You know I know. Looking good, studhoss, looking real good. You and me, we paddled 20 miles a shit creek, huh? Yeah. With our bare hands, we did. Me, I don't forget that. I'm like an elephant, short on smarts, long on memory. You sleep, stud. Ol Megs is on watch. You sleep. (*HE takes off his jacket, drapes it over the sleeping DAVE. HE sits. MARTHA enters in warm, dry clothes.*)

MARTHA. (*crosses to stage left of couch; brings blanket; MEGS stands*) I was so cold. Is he all right?

MEGS. He's in dreamland is all. His head's gonna feel like a bowling alley when he wakes up but he's fine.

MARTHA. He finished off the whole bottle, the poor fool.

MEGS. Guzzled it is what he did. Wasn't the first time, won't be the last. (*HE begins to laugh.*)

MARTHA. What?

MEGS. You. You was a bedraggled cat, woman. You looked like you been on the spin cycle of a washing machine for fourteen hours.

MARTHA. If you hadn't had that blanket in the car I'd have frozen to death.

MEGS. You were terrific, Martha.

MARTHA. Every trout for a hundred miles is probably hiding under a rock in a state of shock.

MEGS. Martha, you fish was gettin away!

MARTHA. Yes I know! But I never thought you'd push me right in after it!

MEGS. I got excited! I mean, I knew you wanted the brainless thing so badly. God . . . he was beautiful, huh Martha? A real rainbow. Hey, if I'da known you was gonna throw down the pole and try haulin him in hand over hand, I'da got you a drop line.

MARTHA. I was startled! I felt as though I'd stepped on a frog. I could feel him through the string.

MEGS. He felt you.

MARTHA. He was heavy.

MEGS. Woman, he was cousin to the Loch Ness monster! Enormous! You got him onto that bank and I thought, look out, Martha! That baby's gonna take your leg off!

MARTHA. No!

MEGS. Yes!!

MARTHA. Really?

MEGS. Hey, would I lie? It's a good thing he threw the hook. He was gettin pissed!

MARTHA. No. He was desperate. My heart went out to him.

MEGS. You're something, Martha. You are. Didn't I tell you there'd be one waitin with your name on it? M-A-R-T-H-A! It was a good time?

MARTHA. (*pause*) It was a wonderful time, Joseph.

MEGS. (*softly*) Yeah? That's just great.

MARTHA. (*MARTHA crosses to kitchen.*) *You* are having some soup.

MEGS. (*MEGS follows.*) *Soup* would be great.

MARTHA. (*MEGS sits chair stage right. MARTHA puts on apron.*) Come on. To the kitchen. Sit. Split pea with ham. Home made.

MEGS. You're kiddin. By god, if food doesn't come out of a can, I usually have a hard time recognizing it.

MARTHA. I'll have you know I'm a very good cook.

MEGS. Well, goddam, we're a team cause I like to eat.

MARTHA. (*MARTHA gets soup from fridge, gets spoon from drawer.*) Do your girlfriends cook for you?

MEGS. Tell you the truth, Martha, most a the girls I know don't know a waffle iron from a frisbee. I been keepin a kinda low profile in the girlfriend department. Got kinda tired of mud wrestlers and hog callers. What about you, Martha? You must have to fight'm off with tomahawks.

MARTHA. (*MARTHA puts soup in pan.*) I'm sorry to inform you I've given up the fight.

MEGS. Come on, woman, you're built like a brick shithouse!

MARTHA. What?

MEGS. Oh, goddam. Me and my mouth again. (*MEGS crosses up right of MARTHA.*) Sorry, Martha, but you are. I noticed it straight off.

MARTHA. That's the most ridiculous thing I've ever heard.

MEGS. No.

MARTHA. I'm shapeless.

MEGS. Solid. You're sturdy. You're a battleship!

MARTHA. Agreed. With the face of an icebreaker.

MEGS. No—oh.

MARTHA. Yes.

MEGS. N—

MARTHA. (*MARTHA puts pan on stove.*) Stop contradicting me! I know what I am. Plain and unattractive.

MEGS. Martha, I saw the picture in there. You used to be.

MARTHA. (*MARTHA clears table dishes to sink. Wipes table with cloth. Crosses to stove, stirs soup.*) You're very nice to try and convince me otherwise but I look in the mirror every morning. I live with what I see. The soup will be ready in a moment.

MEGS. Y'know, Martha, some people, they get awful ugly the minute they open their mouths. And other people, like you, Martha, they grow on you. The more you get to know'm, the better lookin they get.

MARTHA. Very few share your opinion.

MEGS. Oh. You give'm a chance to? (*MEGS sits chair*)

MARTHA. Look, I'm not one of those pieces of fluff you see in men's magazines. Does that make me less a woman? It does not. (*pause*) And I'm a fool because for some stupid reason I think it does. And so I buy contact lenses and clothes I can't really afford. You think I'd of learned by now. You think I'd have learned at the start. (*pause*) The soup is almost hot. (*pause*) David had to even get me a date for my high school formal. I was on the decorations committee, the tickets committee. I put together the whole thing. Nobody asked me to go. David rounded up his friends and told them one of them had to invite me or he'd beat them all up. I think perhaps they drew straws. I didn't know. Suddenly I was invited, that's all that mattered. I was so happy. Well, it was something that couldn't be kept quiet, (*MARTHA crosses downstage stage right of table.*) David's blackmail. I heard rumors. I confronted David. He wouldn't admit what he'd done but I knew. (*pause*)

MEGS. You go? (*pause*)

MARTHA. I got very sick the night of the prom. A 24 hour thing. David meant well.

MEGS. I crashed mine. Yeah, I did. Just walked in wearin a motorcycle jacket, steel-toed jack boots, and shades, stood there like a madman, grinnin at all those tuxedos, hopin somebody'd try to throw me out. I think perhaps I also was very sick on the night of the prom.

MARTHA. Wouldn't we have made a lovely couple. (*crosses to stove, stirs soup*)

MEGS. You'da gone with me?

MARTHA. What?

MEGS. If, y'know, I'da like, asked you, you'da gone with me?

MARTHA. Well . . . yes.

MEGS. Nah.

MARTHA. Yes.

MEGS. Nah.

MARTHA. (*angrily*) Why do you always contradict me? Yes, I would have gone with you.

MEGS. Well, goddam, woman! We'da had a great time!! I can see it! (*HE jumps up, moves to the kitchen door.*) I come to pick you up. I knock on the door. (*HE exits out the door. HE knocks. Bam, Bam, Bam.*)

MARTHA. What are you doing? What are you doing!?

MEGS. (*opening the door, stepping in*) This ain't detention, Martha. It's the prom. Answer the door.

MARTHA. You're in. (*HE realizes that HE is. HE grins. HE shuts the door. HE does a slow spin as if showing off something. Down right.*)

MEGS. Hah!? Hah!?

MARTHA. What?

MEGS. Your mom. She thinks I look very dashing in my tuxedo.

MARTHA. Oh, you do.

MEGS. (*whipping off his hat*) The corsage is as big as a goddam dogwood tree. (*HE tosses his hat into the refrigerator.*) Your father comes over to shake hands. He smells my breath to see if I've been drinking. (*HE exhales.*) I have!

MARTHA. He approves. And offers you an aperitif for the road.

MEGS. Too late! You make your entrance down the stairway! You look . . . terrific!

MARTHA. My gown is silk and gossamer. (*MARTHA crosses down right; MEGS counters.*)

MEGS. Yeah. And you look terrific. Your hair is just so. Hey! Know what it is?

MARTHA. (*breaking the spell*) Preposterous.

MEGS. No! It's beautiful.

MARTHA. My shoes?

MEGS. Listen, you could click your heels three times and they'd take you to Kansas.

MARTHA. Ridiculous.

MEGS. No! (*HE retrieves his hat from the refrigerator.*) There is a moment of embarrassment as I try to pin on your corsage. I am timid.

MARTHA. Of the occasion?

MEGS. Of your gunboats!

MARTHA. (*giggling, slapping at HIM*) Stop! (*SHE takes the hat and puts it on her head, the bill facing backwards.*)

MARTHA. I smile reassuringly. (*SHE does.*)

MEGS. And the air is heavy with the portent of things to come! (*offering his arm*) Shall we go? (*MEGS offers his arm, leads MARTHA centerstage.*)

MARTHA. The chariot awaits?

MEGS. (*HE mimes opening a car door for HER.*) 57 Chevy, roars like a p.t. boat but smooth as glass. In accord with the occasion I have thrown all the empty beer cans in the back seat.

MARTHA. How thoughtful. We arrive?

MEGS. We knock'm dead. You're beautiful.

MARTHA. (*softly*) You're handsome.

MEGS. We dance! (*HE does a ferocious dance: a combination of the jerk and the swim. HE sings the instrumental lead to "En-A-Gada-Da-Vida" by the Iron Butterfly as HE dances.* HE stops, grinning. Then:*) They play a slow one. (*HE begins to sing "Michelle" by the Beatles.* HE opens his arms to HER. SHE comes to HIM. THEY sway.*) What a terrific dancer you are.

MARTHA. (*shyly*) And you.

MEGS. If I step on your feet you give me a shot to the kidneys, o.k.? (*HE pulls HER very close, his hands going down around her waist. SHE stiffens.*)

MARTHA. This is stupid.

MEGS. Just dancing. (*And HE holds HER tighter still*)

MARTHA. (*with a growing terror at his embrace*) Please. Stop it. Get your hands off me! (*SHE struggles*

Note — rights to use this music should be secured by each individual producer from the copyright owner.

*free from HIM, rips the hat from her head, tosses it
away from HER, staggers to the stove. Pause.*)

MEGS. (*MEGS crosses stage left to MARTHA.*)
That's the thing about shy people, Martha. They think
everybody's looking. Nobody is. Cept me. (*unable to
hide his anger, his frustration, his hurt*) And I like what
I see!

MARTHA. For god's sake, sit down. The soup is ready.

MEGS. That bad a dancer, huh! Yeah . . . (*HE moves
to exit out the kitchen door and suddenly, almost
without thinking, HE punches out one of the panes of
glass in the door.*

MARTHA. Joseph!   MEGS. Oh god, I'm
Your hand—   sorry . . .

MEGS. (*MEGS crosses down left to table. MARTHA
crosses stage right of MEGS.*) I'll pay for it, I promise,
oh, I'm so sorry, I'll pay for it. (*And HE is hiding his
hands from HER. SHE is trying to see if they're cut.*)

MARTHA. I don't care about the glass! Is your hand
cut!?

MEGS. No, they're fine! (*And SHE sees the scars on
his hands. Embarrassed, HE tries to hide them. SHE
won't let HIM.*) My hands . . . they ain't so pretty . . .

MARTHA. You've done it before . . .

MEGS. Yeah . . .

MARTHA. Why . . .

MEGS. (*HE pulls hand back, takes hat from counter,
crosses to living room.*) I dunno why, Martha. I'm real
sorry. Listen, you tell Davey so long for me. (*HE starts
to leave, going into the living room, heading for the
front door.*)

MARTHA. Joseph? (*HE stops.*) I'd have wanted you to
take me to the prom. (*pause*)

MEGS. Yeah?

MARTHA. (*softly*) Yes.

MEGS. Really?

MARTHA. (*softly*) Yes. (*pause*) Will you sit and have soup with me? (*pause*)

MEGS. (*MEGS crosses kitchen, sits chair stage right. MARTHA takes bowls and plates from cupboard, fills MEGS bowl with soup, crosses to table, puts soup in front of MEGS.*) Only cause you asked stead a ordered. (*HE enters the kitchen, HE sits. SHE puts a bowl filled with soup in front of HIM.*) Look at this. China. (*looking at the plate the bowl is on*) They match too. I almost got a set a tableware once. Everytime you bought groceries at the store, they gave you a plate. I just didn't shop often enough. (*MARTHA brings spoons and napkins to table.*)

MARTHA. Go on. Start.

MEGS. No, I'm waitin for you. It'll stay hot. I hate eating alone. You eat alone much, Martha? (*MARTHA is getting crackers.*)

MARTHA. (*MARTHA puts soup in bowl.*) Sometime I eat with David. David however, eats alone. (*pause*) I usually correct papers while I eat.

MEGS. Sounds to me like you give out way too much homework, Martha. (*pause*) Sure smells good.

MARTHA. (*MARTHA crosses to chair stage left; sits.*) Thank you.

MEGS. Good as Campbells, I bet. I haven't even tasted it yet and I like it.

MARTHA. Now you can. (*SHE puts her napkin in her lap. HE is on the verge of digging in but notices this. HE puts down his spoon and carefully unfolds his napkin, placing it in his lap. HE tastes his soup. HE tastes it again. Perplexed, yet again. HE grins.*)

MEGS. Good. (*SHE smiles, pleased. THEY eat. Pause.*)

MARTHA. David said you two were in Viet Nam together.

MEGS. Basic right through we were.

MARTHA. He never talks about it.

MEGS. No? Me, I talk about it all the time. To myself when there's no one around to listen. You ever had an ugly melody in your head? You can't get rid of it no matter how hard you try to hum something else.

MARTHA. David gets furious if you even mention it. (*pause*) Did you know David's friend, Bobby?

MEGS. He told you about ol Bobby? Ol Bobby, Martha, he was . . . You take a guy who does something well, he practices, right? Well, ol Bobby, he could just look at it once and do it better right off. Yup. And was he smart? He knew things. But see, he knew'm from here (*tapping his chest*) as well as from here (*tapping his head*). Ol Bobby was our heart. A regular waterwalker. We loved him. Oh, but we was some trio, Bobby, your brother and me. They thought I was lucky. Davey did anyway. Used to. He was alway goin on about how I was a lucky dollar, a rabbit's foot . . . yeah, I ain't foolin. Really! Lucky Megs! (*pause*) That all kinda ended when we lost ol Bobby. It was when, y'know, Davey got hurt and me, I uh . . . I got in the way like I got a habit a doin. Oh, I'll tell you, Martha. Your brother is one sweet bear but Ol Bobby was worth him and me rolled together. (*pause*) You wouldn't a liked me much when I got home. Crazy. I got in fights a lot, dumb ones, five against one where I got the piss kicked out a me. It was not a nice time. And what it got down to was . . . well . . . one night I was lyin around, contemplatin the rafters, wonderin if they could take my weight, and like . . . don't laugh or nothin, please . . . I prayed. I felt better. What was done, was done, y'know? For some reason we'd lost ol Bobby. And it was up to me to make that reason a good one. Cause ol Bobby, he deserved that. I think I've liked myself a little bit more ever since then. (*Pause. MARTHA starts to take the bowls.*)

MEGS. Hey, no way, Jose! Cook doesn't clean. My turn. (*HE takes the bowls to the sink.*)

MARTHA. I think I'm going to cry.

MEGS. Huh?

MARTHA. You make me want to laugh and cry at the same time. I rarely do either one.

MEGS. (*MEGS crosses to stage right chair; pushes it in.*) Oh. Guess I oughta get goin, huh? Sure wish we'd caught some trout. (*HE starts to exit stage left.*)

MARTHA. (*MARTHA stands, crosses stage right.*) You're coming for dinner anyway!

MEGS. (*in disbelief*) I am?

MARTHA. Yes! I'm going to buy steaks and I'm going to make a nice salad and I'm going to put potatoes in the oven and . . . and . . . we'll have wine! I'll get a nice bottle of wine! And pie! I baked a pie this week and we'll put ice cream on it and—Unless of course you have other plans.

MEGS. (*MEGS crosses stage right.*) Are you kiddin me?

MARTHA. Yes?

MEGS. Are you kiddin me?

MARTHA. You'll come?

MEGS. Fuckin A, I'll come! With fuckin bells on! You'll pardon the expression. And listen, I'm buyin the wine!

MARTHA. I don't know wine.

MEGS. Me neither, so what? We'll shoot in the best.

Know why? Cause you and me, Martha, we deserve it! Goddam, I better get cracking! It's gonna take me a year in the shower to get cleaned up and even then I'd hedge my bets!

MARTHA. Eight o'clock?

MEGS. Eight o'clock is good.

MARTHA. I can be ready earlier.

MEGS. Seven thirty is earlier.

MARTHA. How about seven?

MEGS. Goddam, woman! Why don't I just stay and watch you change!? Just kiddin, just kiddin. Opening Day. It feels like Christmas. (*HE puts his lucky hat on MARTHA. MEGS crosses to living room. HE stops on MARTHA'S line.*) I'll be back.

MARTHA. Bye Joseph.

MEGS. Joseph. You're too much, Martha. Something. M-A-R-T-H-A! (*HE exits out the front door, slamming it behind him. MARTHA rushes to the door and peers out watching him go.*)

MARTHA. Oh my . . .

(*DAVID has stirred at the sound of the slamming door. HE sits up on the couch, groggy. A moment. MARTHA turns. SHE and DAVE look at each other. MARTHA is suddenly aware SHE is wearing the hat. SHE quickly takes it off.*)

LIGHT TO BLACK

END OF ACT I

ACT TWO

Scene 1

(*MARTHA enters down the stairs into the living room. SHE is wearing a beautiful dress in a light pastel color, her hair is carefully brushed back, SHE wears a bit of make-up. DAVE enters right behind HER. HE is unchanged, unshaven: is smoking a cigarette.*)

DAVE. What a ya mean you invited him over for dinner?

MARTHA. I thought I spoke English. Invite, a verb, to request the participation of. Dinner. That's a meal if memory serves me. (*MARTHA crosses to stove.*)

DAVE. I don't want to eat dinner with him. (*DAVE crosses to kitchen doorway.*)

MARTHA. Your participation has not been requested. If you'd like to, you may. Go out if you don't. (*MARTHA crosses to couch.*)

DAVE. I don't even want the guy in my house.

MARTHA. It's my house too. What shall we do? Call Mother in Florida and ask for a tie-breaking vote?

DAVE. What is this, Martha? Be kind to stranger week? You don't even know Megs.

MARTHA. (*crosses to magazine rack*) That's why I invited him over. To get to know him.

DAVE. (*crosses centerstage*) What you're going to find out, you don't need.

MARTHA. (*crosses stage right to DAVE; takes cigarette,*

crosses to kitchen, throws it away) David, I am trying to tidy up. It is difficult with you pretending you're Mount St. Helens, spewing ash everywhere. (*MARTHA crosses to sofa; fluffs pillows.*)

DAVE. (*crosses stage left*) Sis, want to know what he was in Viet Nam? Jacknife. That's what he called himself. It's a truckdriving term, sis. It's when you take a big, beautiful 18 wheeler and you crash it, turn it to shit. Jacknife cause he crashed trucks. He was crazy. And Viet Nam made him crazier. He's spent more time in the can on assault charges than you can believe.

MARTHA. (*crosses to trophy case; straightens*) He's been very nice.

DAVE. Nothing's happened to get him started. Push the right button and he's off. Berserk, Martha.

MARTHA. I'm sorry you don't like him, I do.

DAVE. You want to go out with someone? O.k., I'll set you up. Plenty a guys owe me favors, it'll be no problem.

MARTHA. No, thank you.

DAVE. Martha—

MARTHA. (*exiting to the kitchen*) I have to put potatoes in the oven.

DAVE. (*following*) He's nothing but a mechanic, Martha. He owns a garage for christ sake.

MARTHA. And you drive a truck, David. I try not to hold it against you. (*pause*)

DAVE. (*crosses to fridge for beer*) Steak. We were gonna have trout for dinner. What a laugh. I froze my ass off.

MARTHA. I should have thought you were too drunk to feel anything.

DAVE. Martha, listen, I have his number someplace. Call him and tell him something came up, the P.T.A.

MARTHA. Are you joining us?

DAVE. The fucking board of education wants to see you!

MARTHA. Do you want a potato!? (*MARTHA wraps potatoes in foil.*)

DAVE. Yes! (*pause*) If Dad was alive, he wouldn't let a guy like this on the front porch.

MARTHA. Go out, David. Call up your friends, go to a bar and get drunk and hoarse screaming at the television.

DAVE. No way.

MARTHA. Then not another word if you're staying! Be what you usually are, a presence in the house that eats whatever's put in front of it and grunts when spoken to. I'd be better off living with a Saint Bernard!

DAVE. What is with you today?

MARTHA. What do you care, David? Really, why this sudden concern about who I see?

DAVE. Hey, you're my sister.

MARTHA. I thought I was your housekeeper, your cook. I don't know how long it's been since I heard you say, Martha, how are you? I've been invited to a party, come along. Let's get together and do something. How's the old lovelife, kid?

DAVE. What lovelife? You never go out.

MARTHA. Exactly. (*MARTHA gets lettuce from fridge; prepares salad.*)

DAVE. O.k., I'm sorry. I'll take more interest from now on, I really will. Hey, we'll go to a movie. How's that sound? But Martha, forget Megs. The guy is not up to your standards.

MARTHA. Has anyone ever been? My so-called standards, David, are merely something I've hidden behind so I could salvage a little pride. (*pause*) Do you remember that cruise I went on last Easter break?

DAVE. Yeah. You got a nice tan.

MARTHA. It was a swinging singles cruise, a man for every maid. It was a ship filled with depressed, lonely people and I went hoping I might meet . . . what . . . a kindred soul, someone I liked, who liked me, anyone. And I might have. If I could have left my standards at dockside. But I was frightened and so when I went on board my standards walked right up the gangplank behind me. I got a nice tan.

DAVE. Martha, what, you're pissed off you didn't get layed?

MARTHA. Wouldn't you have been?

DAVE. Yeah, but you?

MARTHA. Oh, I'm sorry. Shy, plain women don't desire. When they're in bed at night they keep their hands off themselves and don't fantasize. God . . . (*pause*) David, how many times have you made love?

DAVE. Hey, come on, huh?

MARTHA. Really. Fifteen times? Fifty times? One hundred?

DAVE. Gimme a break.

MARTHA. Good god, David, look at me! I'm almost the perfect image of the virgin school marm. Tending other people's children is supposed to make me feel chaste and noble and fulfilled. Bullshit. I feel helpless and very stupid. I'm not a nun. I wrote boy's names in my notebooks when I was young. I prayed that they'd pull my hair so I'd pay attention to them.

DAVE. Kids don't know shit.

MARTHA. Oh, David, they know. I watch them. Girls are always glancing about. Is anyone looking? Is a boy looking? They are. You call them to the blackboard and they struggle up, bent at the waist, pulling their sweaters down.

DAVE. God, Martha, you checkin out their boners?

MARTHA. You're horrible. I'm just telling you that they know! When you see a boy walking a girl to class, his arm around her, his mouth close to her ear, you know they know. Why should it be too late for me? (*Pause. DAVE suddenly giggles. MARTHA looks at HIM. HE laughs.*)

MARTHA. (*annoyed*) What?

DAVE. (*HE stands upstage of center chair.*) Uh . . . Before. About being a virgin school marm? You said almost. I mean, I never thought that you . . . uh, it never occurred to me that . . . (*HE laughs.*) Who'd you get it on with? Anybody I know?

MARTHA. (*puts salad in fridge; gets flour out*) You just . . . that's none of your business.

DAVE. Yeah, it is. Come on. Please?

MARTHA. (*gets flower vase from top of fridge*) Go away.

DAVE. Martha, I'm curious. Martha? Mar—tha? (*HE is laughing openly now.*)

MARTHA. Leave me alone. (*crosses to right chair*)

DAVE. Loosen the strings, sis. Come on, gossip a little. (*pause*)

MARTHA. Wiliam Green.

DAVE. Ichabod Crane? I don't believe it. (*HE laughs harder than ever.*)

MARTHA. That's why it's so hard for people like me. People like you make fun of someone's rear end or waist line. You turn love into a beauty pageant. Stop laughing! (*SHE arranges flowers.*)

DAVE. (*trying to stop but not succeeding*) No! No! It's not cause a the way you look. (*HE sits.*)

MARTHA. Oh!

DAVE. It's just that . . . I mean, you're not what you'd call experienced. Are you? (*HE laughs.*) No! And him . . . he was a shy guy and well . . . (*HE laughs.*) Laurel and Hardy! This is another fine mess you've got me into! (*HE laughs.*)

MARTHA. Oh David, I could have died. Neither of us knew what we were doing. We were like two cars that had hooked bumpers . . . both of pushing and pulling at the wrong times. And he kept apologizing the whole time. I'm terribly sorry. I think he hoped I'd change my mind. (*THEY laugh.*) I don't know why I'm laughing . . . It was horrible. No passion. Guilt for him. Frustrated tears for me.

DAVE. (*tenderly*) I'm sorry, kiddo.

MARTHA. He asked me to marry him. He'd been in bed with me so he thought he should.

DAVE. (*considering this a moment*) Y'know, he wasn't such a bad guy.

MARTHA. (*bristling*) Meaning I won't get many chances? Meaning I'm not in any position to pick and choose?

DAVE. Here you go again. (*rises; crosses to sink*)

MARTHA. I didn't sleep with him so he'd marry me. We'd have made each other miserable. (*pause*) Are you having dinner with us?

DAVE. Sis, you make dinner for Megs, he'll latch onto you. He'll be calling, coming by, telling me all sorts of crazy stuff. We won't be able to get rid of him. You're making a mistake. Martha.

MARTHA. It's my mistake then.

DAVE. Jesus, Martha, why won't you listen to me?!
Do you know anything about men? No! You'd have a
hard time handling the most perfect son of a bitch in the
world let alone this guy! (*pause*) All right. All right.
You'll see. You'll be beggin him to leave. (*MARTHA
rises; crosses to sink; puts water in vase*)

MARTHA. Go get cleaned up. You'll feel better.
(*pause*)

DAVE. (*softly*) Is it really so bad here, Martha?

MARTHA. It's not so bad. (*SHE gets tablecloth from
drawer.*)

DAVE. I love this place. Every good memory I have is
here. (*pause*) I like having you around here, Martha.
(*pause*) Listen, I'm gonna be more appreciative, you'll
see.

MARTHA. The things I want, you can't give me,
David.

DAVE. You're gonna leave?

MARTHA. Some day. (*puts tablecloth on table; long
pause*) Go get cleaned up.

DAVE. Yeah. I got any clean clothes anywhere?

MARTHA. In the dryer.

DAVE. (*preoccupied*) Get'm for me, huh? (*HE exits
upstairs. MARTHA puts the finishing touches on her
table. MEGS comes to the front door. HE has flowers
which HE hides behind his back. HE is carrying a large
bag.*)

MEGS. (*knocking*) Hello, it's me! Front door! (*SHE
scurries around, checking everything to make sure it's
perfect. SHE checks her reflection in one of the windows. SHE hurries to the door, pauses, takes a deep
breath, lets HIM in.*)

MARTHA. Well now.

MEGS. Just a pack horse, that's me. (*HE displays the flowers, surprising HER.*)

MARTHA. Oh, my.

MEGS. Like'm? I told the guy I was a white knight going to meet a fair damsel. Give me your best!

MARTHA. They're beautiful.

MEGS. Wait. Here.

MARTHA. No!

MEGS. Yes! Candy.

MARTHA. Ohh . . .

MEGS. Just a mad seducer, that's me. I got wine too. No idea what goes with what so I got one of every color; white, pink and blood red. And . . . this!

MARTHA. Brandy?

MEGS. If beer for breakfast is sunrise, brandy is sundown. (*And doing a quick "bump and grind", HE takes off his overcoat. HE is wearing a very well-made, dark three-piece suit, a white shirt, a tie.*)

MARTHA. Look at you.

MEGS. It looked real good in the store window. I hardly ever get to wear it. I figured what the hell, prom night, y'know? (*pause*) I'm real glad to be here, Martha. (*SHE hestitates, then leans up and kisses HIM on the cheek.*)

LIGHTS GO TO BLACK.

ACT TWO

SCENE 2

(*MEGS and MARTHA are in the kitchen. Dinner has*

been finished. MEGS has taken off his jacket, loosened his tie, rolled up his sleeves. HE sits at the table and sips wine. MARTHA is putting the finishing touches on clean-up.)

MEGS. Martha, I feel like I fell asleep and woke up in the Waldorf Astoria.

MARTHA. Go on.

MEGS. I do. Steaks I usually eat are so bad, you put'm down knowin the restaurant's gotta make up for it by given you all the beer you can drink. (*pause*) Come on, Martha you sit down.

MARTHA. Joseph— (*MEGS takes apron off MARTHA, puts it on, puts MARTHA in center chair.*)

Megs. Hush, hush, hush. Sit. Have another glass of this Parisian nectar. (*pours*) I'm finishing up here. I'm not taking no for an answer. These hands may finger-paint in axle grease by day but come nightfall they whisper messages to me. Clean us, Megs. Drown us in boraxo. Wash the bathtub or something. So I do. My hands like it.

MARTHA. You're a funny man.

MEGS. (*crosses to sink*) I am, ain't I? Aren't. Aren't I. Good wine?

MARTHA. Oh yes. I heartily approve. (*giggling*) Listen to me. Such an expert. The tip of my nose has gone numb. I'll be swinging from the chandeliers next. Oh, I want to wrap the steak in tin foil for you so you can take it home. (*rises; crosses to counter*)

MEGS. Hey, no way, Jose! That's teacher's lunch for two days.

MARTHA. You're taking it.

MEGS. Oh, god, I'm being ordered again. How can I refuse.

MARTHA. You can't.

MEGS. Are you sure?

MARTHA. (*wrapping steak*) I try not to eat lunch. You saw my picture in there. The Hindenberg. My idea of an exceptional Saturday night used to be two pounds of fudge and thirty term papers. I've finally eliminated the two pounds of fudge.

MEGS. And from all the right places too. (*pause*)

MARTHA. This will be in the refrigerator. Don't you forget it either. More wine?

MEGS. You?

MARTHA. Yes.

MEGS. Me too. (*HE pours them more wine.*)

MARTHA. Why don't you take the wine in the living room and get comfortable. I'll be there in a moment. (*MEGS enters the living room. MARTHA prepares a tray for the brandy: a cloth, snifters. MEGS is at the trophy case looking at MARTHA's picture when DAVE comes downstairs.*)

MEGS. Hey, some dinner. Can your sister cook?

DAVE. (*crosses between chair and couch*) Not bad.

MEGS. Come on, stud, your idea a cooking is to throw the meat in the pan, turn the flame on high and go and take a shower.

DAVE. Yeah . . . (*DAVE moves to the kitchen.*)

MEGS. (*crosses to DAVE*) Hey! Listen, if she asks for my references, lie! Hah!? Hah!? (*And HE punches DAVE affectionately in the belly. MEGS crosses to tropy case. DAVE enters the kitchen. HE gets a beer from the ice box.*)

MARTHA. (*gets snifters from cupboard*) It's going very well, don't you think?

DAVE. Your steak was pretty good. A little rare for my tastes.

MARTHA. You seem to be enjoying yourself.

DAVE. I didn't think either of you knew I was here. This is great, Martha. Terrific, Martha. Look at you, Martha. And you eating it up. I didn't know who to laugh at.

MEGS. Hey, team captain, big number 50, like Butkus!

DAVE. Enthusiastic, isn't he.

MARTHA. (*crosses with flowers to counter*) Positive. Optimistic. It's refreshing. (*pause*)

DAVE. He's a loser. (*Pause. And MARTHA suddenly slams an open drawer shut with a loud bang.*)

MARTHA. You're the loser, David. Ever since you came home. What is it like to aspire to nothing more than getting drunk on Saturday night?

DAVE. I aspire to be left the fuck alone!

MARTHA. By what? Life in general? Why even be a human being, David?

DAVE. Good question.

MARTHA. The idea of anyone finding anything, even for a moment offends you, you selfish—

DAVE. (*overlapping*) I want you to see what he's like! (*crosses to MARTHA.*)

MARTHA. I know what he's like. He's gentle and he's kind and we're having a wonderful time. He likes me. You didn't have to threaten to beat him up if he didn't.

DAVE. What?

MARTHA. The time you got me the prom date!

DAVE. Oh, god . . .

MARTHA. That was done out of generosity and love, feelings you've forgotten about. You're willing to keep me in this house just so it won't be empty on the rare occasions you decide to come home! Well, I'm moving, David. I'm leaving! Like Mother! All the tears she shed!

Did you really think all of them were for Poppa? Most of them were for you! YOU MIGHT AS WELL HAVE BEEN DEAD TOO! (*crosses to table for brandy and snifters*)

DAVE. How'd you like a slap in the mouth!?

MARTHA. I—dare—you! (*And picking up her tray SHE exits to the living room.*)

DAVE. (*crosses to doorway*) You're a shrew, Martha! You got the face of a football cleat and could use a series of shots for distemper! Him tellin you different doesn't make it so! It doesn't make it so!

MEGS. (*crosses down right to DAVE*) You shouldn't, Davey.

DAVE. I shouldn't what!?

MEGS. Talk to someone who loves you like that, you shouldn't.

DAVE. I want you to tell me something, man—

MARTHA. You don't have to tell him anything, Joseph—

DAVE. He does! Just what are you doin, huh? You plannin on being lucky for my sister!? Like you were for me? Like you were for Bobby?

MARTHA. Just leave, David.

DAVE. He knows what I'm talking about.

MEGS. What bugs you, man. That you thought I was lucky? Or that you was so piss-assed scared, you grabbed hold a that luck like it was rosary beads?

DAVE. I'd give anything to know why it's your face I'm staring at and not Bobby's.

MEGS. Get fucked. (*crosses stage right to kitchen*)

DAVE. He loved it, Martha! He ate it up! Get some! Get some a them gooks! Bap-bap-bap-bap-bap-bap! Blow'm away! Nothin confusion about that, huh Jacknife?

MEGS. It was heartbreaking the things I did. I'll live my whole life being sorry for'm —

DAVE. But you loved it! You never had it so good. It was logical to you. And you just had to carry Bobby and me right along with you.

MEGS. Not Bobby, man. Bobby understood.

DAVE. Bobby is dead! Man! When you gonna remember that!?

MEGS. You fuckin jocks . . . (*Crosses to living room; crosses up left to trophy case. And suddenly HE blows. HE is at the trophy case and with a sweep of his hand HE sends trophies careening into the wall.*) You and your fucking jock dreams! I was a truckdriving numb-nuts and they drafted me! But you!

DAVE. Yeah!?

MEGS. He enlisted. Mr. High School Hero enlisted! Went marchin off thinkin those piranha-eyed, cheese-faced motherfuckers was gonna tackle you stead a blow you away!!

DAVE. Jacknife set me straight!

MEGS. I stayed alive the only way I could! I rooted in what was happening around me like a pig in shit! And you ain't gonna blame me or make me feel guilty no more!

DAVE. Thirty feet off the ground in a chopper, Martha, and he's screaming like a rabid dog to get lose!

MEGS. Yeah! And you so close to lucky Megs, I thought you was tryin to cornhole me, man! No way, Megs. I can't, Megs! Not in a million, Megs! NEVER HAPPEN!

DAVE. (*overlapping*) We shoulda stayed put, mother-fucker. We should have stayed! But we went! Cause a you!

MEGS. Me and Bobby had to throw him out of the

helicopter, Martha! Commanding officer was threaten-
ing to shoot him!

DAVE. Bullshit!

MEGS. You chickenshit. I heard you, Davey.

DAVE. You heard what?

MEGS. (*crosses to DAVE*) I heard. You was scared
and tight and you landed wrong and your ankles broke.
Bobby and I came back for you. I got hit cause a that.
And I lay there in the mud with the blood pumpin from
my chest, blurp-blurp, and I heard you. No, Bobby!
Don't go back for him! Fuck Megs! Jacknife is dead!
Don't go back for him, Bobby! But Bobby did go back,
huh Davey? (*DAVE exits up left. MEGS follows up
left.*) You can't walk away from that! Bobby did go
back! Davey!? Bobby did! BOBBY DID! (*Pause. Then
softly, through tears.*) Bobby did . . . (*Pause. Crosses
stage right upstage of couch.*) Maybe we never shoulda
jumped outta that helicopter. Shootaway, sir. All of us,
we don't give a fuck! Dead or alive, we're stayin right
here! No way we're goin down into that shit! Hindsight.
(*Sits in chair. Pause.*)

MARTHA. (*Crosses right to MEGS. softly.*) Joseph?

MEGS. Mmm?

MARTHA. Let's got out and do something wonderful.
(*pause*)

MEGS. Whatcha got in mind, you mad miss.

MARTHA. (*pause*) I'd like to see your gas station.
(*pause*) And we'll go by my school after. I'll show you
where I work. I have keys. I could show you my
classroom. Charts on the wall . . . tick-tack-toe on the
blackboard. (*pause*) Shall I get my coat? (*pause*)

MEGS. O.k. (*MARTHA crosses to kitchen; turns off
lights; checks stove; crosses to living room. SHE gets
their coats. SHE puts her own on, helps HIM into his.*

MEGS crosses up left.) Sneakin back into high school, Martha. If I don't feel notorious or something. (*pause*)
MARTHA. I'll protect you, Joseph.

LIGHTS TO BLACK AS THEY
EXIT OUT THE FRONT DOOR

ACT TWO

SCENE 3

(*It is several hours later. MEGS and MARTHA enter through the kitchen door. There is a somberness, a preoccupation to MEGS that MARTHA is trying desperately to fight. MEGS is carying a case of soda in his arms. HE holds the door for MARTHA.*)

MARTHA. Thank you. And thank you for the gasoline.
MEGS. (*crosses to kitchen, puts soda on counter*) Better you than the A-rabs, Martha.
MARTHA. I like my case of soda too. Thank you very much for that.
MEGS. You're welcome. (*crosses stage left*)
MARTHA. A whole case of white birch beer. What am I going to do with that? (*pause*) I suppose I could bathe in it. (*takes off coat*)
MEGS. You don't want it, Martha, I'll take it back.
MARTHA. Joseph, no, I'm teasing.
MEGS. Oh.

MARTHA. (*crosses to coat rack*) You tease me unmercifully and then you can't tell when you're being teased.

MEGS. Sorry.

MARTHA. (*crosses to MEGS; takes his coat; crosses up left*) Teasing, it shows you're cared for, doesn't it? (*pause, he doesn't respond, then softly*) I think it does. (*pause*) Do you know what white birch beer is, Joseph?

MEGS. (*crosses up left of living room chair*) No.

MARTHA. (*crosses to couch stage right*) I'll tell you if you'd like.

MEGS. Please.

MARTHA. Snow covered trees in a bottle. (*pause*) Joseph, what's the matter? You're with me and then you're not with me.

MEGS. Sorry.

MARTHA. You were hoping he'd be home, weren't you. He's not your friend, Joseph.

MEGS. I'm his friend.

MARTHA. (*pause*) You're a lovely man. I mean that.

MEGS. No, you don't.

MARTHA. I do and you are.

MEGS. I got big bulgy eyes.

MARTHA. Well . . .

MEGS. And I am sorta losin my hair.

MARTHA. That's a sign of virility, Joseph.

MEGS. Whoa.

MARTHA. You have a wonderful, open smile.

MEGS. I do not.

MARTHA. You do.

MEGS. (*crosses to MARTHA*) You're just leadin me on woman, so's you can get into my panties.

MARTHA. Now you're teasing me.

MEGS. Hey, it shows you're cared for. (*Pause. It*

seems THEY are almost going to kiss.) Martha, let's go look for him.

MARTHA. (*desperately*) He's not worth your concern. (*pause*) Please. Let's have our brandy. (*Crosses to couch, sits; MEGS crosses to couch. SHE moves to pour. SHE is stopped by the sound of DAVE entering. There is blood on his face and hands. His shirt is open and there is blood on his T-shirt. His eye is discolored and swollen. HE moves as if HE is in a daze. Crosses to center of doorway arch; MEGS stands. Long silence.*)

DAVE. (*softly*) I . . . uh . . . I fell down.

MEGS. How's the ground look, stud? (*pause*)

DAVE. Martha . . . (*crosses to up left of couch*)

MARTHA. What? You want someone to tend your wounds? I'm sorry, David, not tonight. (*Pause. DAVE wants to say something, cannot.*)

MEGS. Want some ice for that eye, Davey?

DAVE. (*softly*) Martha, I'm sorry . . . (*pause*)

MEGS. (*crosses to DAVE; leads him stage right to chair; takes out handkerchief, kneels*) Come on, guy, sit. Let's see what you look like under all that blood. Don't worry, it's clean. You know me, I have to wipe my nose, I use my sleeve. (*HE wipes at DAVE's mouth.*) Hold on. (*pause*) How can she understand, stud? She doesn't know. She wasn't there. (*pause*) Hey, we hardly beat you home, guy. Yeah, we been out. I showed Martha my garage. It's just a garage and all but I put a case a pop in her arms so it turned out o.k. You want a birch beer, Davey? Good pop. (*silence*) Maybe Martha'd make us some coffee. (*MARTHA doesn't move.*) Then we went and saw Martha's classroom. Whoo, stud, beakers and specimens and microscopes. All we needed was a lightning bolt and we coulda created a monster. And we woulda nicknamed him Davey.

DAVE. (*softly*) Jacknife.

MEGS. (*MARTHA crosses to kitchen; to sink.*) That's my name, don't wear it out. That's what Bobby called me.

DAVE. Cause you drove the trucks.

MEGS. I did. Crashed a lot of the mothers too. (*pause; crosses to kitchen doorway*) Why don't you tell Martha what your nickname was. I bet she'd like to know. (*pause*) No? I will then. High School! Cause he loved high school. You was all league and you loved high school. Maybe too much, huh? Ol Bobby had a nickname for everything, didn't he? (*pause*) Huh? Tell Martha how Bobby could make it seem like boy scouts sitting around the campfire. Couldn't he do that? (*pause*) He could, Martha. (*MARTHA fills kettle, puts it on stove, stands. Pause. And it is as if MEGS is suddenly making a decision. Crosses to living room down left.*) When I first got back, Davey, and was drivin, I'd see old Bobby standin at the side of the road with his thumb out. Isn't that something? It'd be late at night maybe and I'd be tired and I'd blink my eyes and there he'd be, standing there in his combat fatigues. Lotta people think they understand what that's like, don't they, studhoss. Well, god love'm for bad liars. They can only try. You and me, we know it like it was yesterday morning. Know what else, Davey? Sometimes I'd even pick ol Bobby up. (*DAVE groans softly.*) You believe that? I swear, one time Bobby sat next to me from Pittsburgh, PA, all the way to Hartford, Connecticut. Wasn't a bad conversation either. You ever do that? Pick'm up? Davey? Did ya? Davey, did you ever do that?

MARTHA. (*crosses to center chair; sits*) David, did you ever do that?

DAVE. (*softly*) Oh, god, Martha . . .

MEGS. You did, didn't you. What'ja think? Scare ya? Nah. Nothin scary about ol Red Sock. That was Bobby's nickname, Martha. Cause he loved the Red Soxs. Didn't he Davey? Huh? Ol Bobby? (*crosses to stage right of couch, kneels*)

DAVE. He was gonna take us to Fenway Park . . . We were gonna cheer . . . Oh, Bobby . . . You shoulda stayed put. You shouldn't have gone back. Bobby didn't help you, Megs.

MEGS. Died reaching down for me. Opened up like a rose in front a my eyes. Never knew what hit him.

DAVE. If he'd stayed, he would of lived!

MEGS. Guy, how many nights have I stared at the ceiling thinkin that very thought. But he didn't stay put. Wasn't in him to leave me any more'n it was to leave you!

DAVE. If I hadn't been scared, if I hadn't landed wrong—

MEGS. Guy, things happen for a reason!

DAVE. What reason!?

MEGS. I ain't sure. I'm only workin on it.

DAVE. Then how come you're doin so much better than me!?

MEGS. Davey . . . I been blamin myself for things I have no control over since first light. The way I look . . . way I talk . . . way I act . . . I was never no high school hero. I didn't have so far to fall.

DAVE. (*so tired*) I just want to be left alone. I want Bobby to leave me alone.

MEGS. Embrace him, stud. Take him in your arms. You and me, we got enough shithole memories to last a lifetime. He ain't one of'm. He was our friend. Our heart. A waterwalker. Did we love him? (*pause*) What were we gonna do, when we got back, no matter what? (*pause*) Come on. Help me, no matter what.

DAVE. I dunno.

MEGS. Yeah, ya do. Come on. We were gonna . . . Davey!

DAVE. I dunno, go to Fenway Park!

MEGS. Best seats in the house, huh? Huh?

DAVE. Hot dogs and beer.

MEGS. And that green grass fresh mowed.

DAVE. The sun beating down.

MEGS. Take off our shirts, huh? Soak up some rays!

DAVE. And we were gonna cheer. Cheer for Bobby's favorite team.

MEGS. Cheer so loud, they was gonna start cheerin us back, yeah. And then?

DAVE. And then we were gonna . . . (*HE stops.*)

MEGS. What, Davey? (*pause*) What?

DAVE. Go fishing . . . Opening day. (*A silence. DAVE settles back in his chair, exhausted. MEGS moves away, lost in his own thoughts now. MEGS crosses down left.*) Martha?

MARTHA. Yes?

DAVE. I got in a fight tonight.

MARTHA. I know you did.

DAVE. With kids. The bar was filled with kids in high school letter sweaters, barely 18, if they were at all, and I dunno . . . I'd look at them, Sis, and it was bringing tears to my eyes looking at them and finally I couldn't any more and I started pushing one of them. He looked scared. But he pushed back and when he did I just sorta waded into all of them. And christ, Martha . . . they didn't know how to fight . . . they didn't know how to fight at all. I don't know what to do. I think I might have hurt one of them. Maybe they're still there. Maybe I should go back and see if he's all right. (*HE stands.*)

MARTHA. Maybe you should.

DAVE. I will. (*Crosses up left. HE moves to the front door. HE stops and turns.*) I blame people. I blame people so goddam much. (*pause*) I'm so sorry, Martha . . .

MARTHA. I know you are. (*HE turns to leave. HE sees Bobby's lucky hat hanging by the door. Pause. HE puts on the hat. HE turns and looks at MEGS. Pause. HE exits. Silence. MEGS moves to the window, watches DAVE go off into the night.*)

MEGS. It's snowing. Awful late in the year. Real pretty. Last gasp. (*pause*) It's hard. Martha, sweet, Martha, it's so god-fuckin hard to put the fatigues to sleep. . . (*Pause. HE moves to leave. MEGS crosses up left to coats.*)

MARTHA. You're leaving.

MEGS. Thought I would. Let things get back to normal.

MARTHA. Has normal been succeeding so well?

MEGS. Your brother loves you, Martha. Well . . .

MARTHA. (*crosses to kitchen doorway*) We never had brandy, Joseph.

MEGS. You're right. We didn't.

MARTHA. One glass. We deserve it.

MEGS. Shoot it in. (*MEGS crosses to stage right of couch; MARTHA crosses to downstage couch. SHE pours, THEY drink.*) Sundown. (*HE moves to leave. MEGS puts glass down; crosses to coat; opens front door.*)

MARTHA. (*crosses stage right; back to MEGS, in despair*) Stay? (*pause*) We'll go upstairs.

MEGS. What's there?

MARTHA. (*inaudibly*) Bedrooms. (*clearing her throat*) Bedrooms.

MEGS. (*crosses to stage right of couch; not unkindly*)
Who the fuck we kiddin, Martha?

MARTHA. Mission accomplished, is that it?

MEGS. A woman like you, a madman like me, who we
kiddin but ourselves?

MARTHA. (*crosses stage left*) You brought me flowers
and candy and wine. We were having a wonderful time.

MEGS. One a the best I ever had, Martha, but—

MARTHA. It doesn't have to end. If I've been fooling
myself, I can fool myself a little longer.

MEGS. I can't, Martha. (*HE exits. Silence. Very slowly,
as if SHE's afraid SHE might break, MARTHA sits.
Silence. MEGS enters in a rush, closing the door quickly
behind. MARTHA rises; crosses stage right.*) Y'know, I
bet we woulda left that prom dance early!

MARTHA. Do you think?

MEGS. (*crosses stage right*) Yeah! We woulda gone off
for dinner at a fancy restaurant! Partridge maybe!

MARTHA. Partridge?

MEGS. (*crosses to up center*) Can't have cheeseburgers,
woman! And then maybe we woulda driven someplace.
Someplace quiet. And parked. And then . . . who
knows!? (*Pause. And the false bravado falls away.
Softly*) Who knows . . . (*pause*) I'm real nervous,
Martha.

MARTHA. (*crosses to MEGS*) It's prom night. We've
been kissing and hugging in the back of your '57 Chevy
for hours. And we've had brandy. (*pause*) Let's go
upstairs. (*SHE takes his hand.*) It's time. (*As THEY go
up the stairs, the lights go to black.*)

END OF PLAY

PROPERTY PLOT

PRESET – ONSTAGE – KITCHEN (all light switches down)

Standing counter/cupboard

two new white candles
foil } left drawer

white linen table cloth   right drawer

silver tray with
  colander on salad bowl } left cupboard

platter with steak
bowl-vase } right cupboard
mixing bowl/measuring cup

Ironing board (between frig. and counter)

Sink Cupboards (5 above L-R)

#1 dressing
   dishes
#2 (top)
   old wine glasses, candle holders – silver
#2 (bottom)
   3 dinner plates
#3 (top)
   3 water glasses (dressing)
   3 juice glasses
#3 (bottom)
   2 soup bowls
   2 soup liners

#4 (top)
    dressing — glasses
    small tumbler
#4 (bottom)
    4 coffee mugs
    sugar/creamer
#5 saltines
    can of drip coffee (¼ full)

Sink Cupboards (on top L-R)

Mixer
Cookie/Candy Box } dressing
Iron
3 brandy snifters (in box)
Large soup tureen — dressing

Trash Can (full of beer cans)

Broom and Dustpan

Kitchen Table (covered with oilcloth)
3 Kitchen chairs at table

Refrigerator (top shelf)

½ carton milk
½ carton o.j.
½ container pea soup (heated)
dozen eggs
3 potatoes
½ head lettuce, torn, in plastic bag
maple syrup

Refrigerator (bottom shelf)

Flowers in florist paper
spare beer

Refrigerator (on top)

message board on downstage side
canister set
recipe card box

Sink Couner (L-R)

Beige Napkins (at least 4)
Toaster
Hand lotion
Blue towel (on hook)
Dish drying rack (w/top parts coffee pot)
Dish towels (3) hanging on hooks
(over counter—paper towel rack, can opener, 4 trivets
  on hooks)

Stove

spice rack over stove
potholders (3) hang on hooks above
teapot
bottom half of drip coffee pot (w/hot cof)

Sink Drawers (3 L-R top)

#1 prop towels
    extra napkins *apron on hook below #1*
#2 3 spoons
    3 soup spoons
    dressing (knives/forks)

#3 1 wooden spoon
    1 plastic spoon
    salad servers — wooden

Sink Cupboards (under, L-R)
#1 wooden bowl — dressing
#2 frying pan
    sauce pan
#3 dressing — cookie sheets
            muffin pan

PRESET — ONSTAGE — Living Room (all light switches
    down)

Chair
Ottoman
Couch with 3 pillows
Magazine Rack — 2 magazines on top
                magazines on shelf
                beer can at up right leg
Telephone table — phone book/phone on top
                small calendar hanging over
                table on wall
3 Rugs — 2 small throw, 1 oriental
2 Coats — hung at front door wall (Martha's good coat
    and Dave's fatigue)

Trophy Shelves (3)

Top — 5 miscellaneous trophies
    — pictures (L-R) Glynnis, 2 football team, Martha

Middle (L-R)

"all league" plaque

wooden trophy-box
pictures of football team, wrestling team, Mom and
   Dad, Unknown woman
interspersed 4 miscellaneous trophies
beer can

Bottom (L-R)

3 trophies, tallest to shortest (broken each show)
large conch shell
wooden box radio

Top of the entire case — 4 old large trophies

Trophy cupboards (underneath) L-R

#1 whiskey bottle — ½ full
    filler bottles, glasses
    basket   bottom shelf
    dressing — magazines   top shelf
#2 empty
#3 empty

PRESET-OFFSTAGE LEFT

by front door porch railing — 3 cans
on milk crate

prop area

white stool
2 six packs cold beer — one opened
case of birch beer
makeup shelf w/makeup, blood

PRESET—OFFSTAGE RIGHT

draped blanket
behind back porch wall—bag for broken glass

PRESET—BACKSTAGE CENTER

full/primed hudson sprayer
drain bucket
grocery bag w/3 wines, brandy,
        flowers, candy } under upcenter stairs
towel draped on stair railing
bowl of water on shelf over stairs

PERSONAL—MARTHA

golf club
glasses

PERSONAL—MEGS

worms } in fishing vest
fly

SCENE ACTIVITY

During Scene I   remove full beer can—Martha
                        empty out beer can—Martha

During Scene II   *Prep for Intermission Changes*
                        plastic wash basin
                        plastic bag—for grounds
                        garbage bag—for beer cans

                        for presetting—bloody t-shirt
                                  and denim shirt
                            —wet paper towels

Intermission—
person #1

KITCHEN
{
bring out tub, clear all used
    dishes, pans, silverware
bring back all dishes, pans,
    silverware *washed* pans under-
    neath, rest to drying rack
take off remaining: mixing
    bowl, creamer, measuring cup
}

OFFSTAGE
{
take to offstage left: bloody
    t-shirt, denim shirt, bag with
    3 wines, brandy, candy,
    flowers, wet paper towels
take stool out at left
take covers off makeup on shelf
remove: costumes, beer
}

FRONT DOOR
COAT RACK
{
return fatigue to coat rack (get
    from David)
put Meg's baseball hat on coat
    rack (get from Martha)
}

person #2

KITCHEN
{
bring on plastic bag and apron
    (get from Martha)
remove ⅔ beer cans from trash
    can—strike in bag
clean up glass from floor and
    window
strike syrup, milk in creamer to
    frig.
put beer and flowers in florist
    paper to top shelf of frig.
strike flour from mixing bowl
    back into canister
strike measuring cup, creamer
    (empty) and bowl (to #1)
bring out short vase from
    counter cupboard—to frig. top
potatoes from frig. to stove top
}

LIVING ROOM {
  1 beer can and glass to trophy case
  pick up towel, blanket, and red sweatshirt from couch-strike
  put green chair back on spike mark
  shove ottoman upstage to couch
}

KITCHEN {
  wipe off counters, table
  strike David's wool shirt jacket from floor (off right)
  strike golf club
}

End of Intermission

(put away all struck props, costumes)

During Scene III   Prep for BO change into Scene IV

person #2   Rose bottle with 2 inches rose
(kitchen)   2 glasses — 1 with dash of rose
                       2 half burned candles

person #1   vase
(liv. rm.)

BO CHANGE SC 3 INTO 4
LIGHTS OUT

Megs and Martha go from L Room to kitchen
    take brandy to kitchen counter (Megs)
    leave candy on phone table
    leave flowers on green chair

#1 enters through closet door
    pick flowers from chair — put in vase on mag. rack
    remove bag with wines (strike)
    exit through closet door — to headphones

#2 enters through porch false wall
    put wine glasses, rose on table

exchange new candles with burned ones
take steak/platter out from under side counter to
  top of counter
take brandy from sink counter — to top side counter
exit out false wall in porch

Martha takes potatoes out of oven and put in sink puts
on apron
Megs goes to kitchen chair right, removes coat, sits

LIGHTS UP

During Scene IV and V
                    Put away all props, costumes
                    possible.

AFTER CURTAIN   Strike Act II props, restore all
                    food props to refrig.

COSTUME PLOT

ACT I, Scene 1

MARTHA
Eyeglasses
Dk. Blue Bathrobe
Lt. Blue Flannel Nightgown
Lt. Blue Slippers

Chinos
Red Paid Flannel Shirt
Belt — Leather
Red Kerchief
Beige-Tan Jacket
L.L. Bean Boots
Beige Socks

MEGS
White Winter Undershirt
Red, Green & Yellow Plaid Flannel
    Shirt
Faded Red Sweatshirt
Tan Fishing Vest
Blue Jeans
Work Boots
Leather Belt
Work Socks
Boston Red Soxs Baseball Cap

DAVID
Pale Blue Boxer Shorts
White Athletic Socks

Blue Athletic T-Shirt
Blue Jeans
Leather Belt

Sneakers
Brown CPO Shirt
Fatigue Jacket

Scene 2

MARTHA   Maroon Plaid Skirt
              Maroon Sweater — Pullover
              Nylons
              Brown Loafers

ACT II Scene 3

MARTHA   Pink Dress
              Pink Belt
              Pink Sandals — Med. Heel
              Nylons
              Beige Coat

MEGS   Navy 3-Piece Suit
              White Shirt
              Dk. Blue & Maroon Tie
              Black Shoes
              Black Socks
              Dk. Belt
              White Handkerchief
              Beige Wool Overcoat

DAVID   White T-Shirt
              Blue Work Shirt
              Brown Corduroy Pants
              Brn. Boots
              Brn. Belt
              Duplicate of Work Shirt & T-Shirt
                  both stained w/Blood

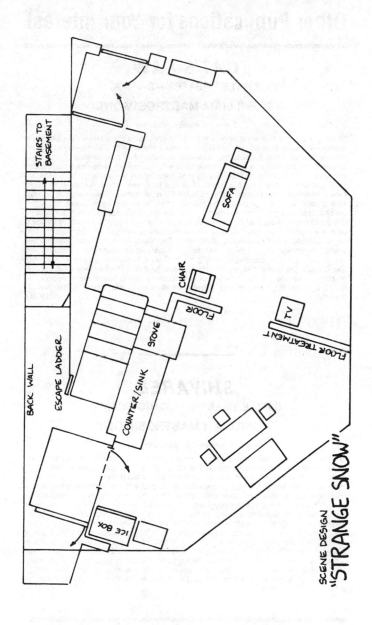

SCENE DESIGN
"STRANGE SNOW"

CAT'S PAW
(LITTLE THEATRE—DRAMA)
By WILLIAM MASTROSIMONE
2 men, 2 women—Interior

This is a gripping drama about terrorism; but it does not come at the subject in a way you'd expect. When we think of "the terrorist", we generally think of a wild-eyed religious or political fanatic. What if, posits the acclaimed author of *The Woolgatherer*, *Extremities*, *Shivaree* and *Nanawatai*, a terrorist came along who was brilliant, who was articulate and who was *right*? Victor is the head of a terrorist group which is responsible for a bomb attack against the White House in which 27 people have been killed. He has arranged to have a television news reporter led to his lair, there to tell the world why he has done what he has done. Victor's obsession is the destruction of the world's water supply, and with it the final destruction of the human race, by pollution. When the reporter asks him if he feels any guilt about the death of the 27 innocent people, he replies that hundreds of innocent people are dying every hour because of what mankind is doing to its water supply—and do the people responsible feel guilt for this? This cat-and-mouse game between the young woman reporter and Victor gets more and more tense, leading to a shocking and violent conclusion. A standing-room-only hit at Seattle Repertory Theatre and later at San Diego's Old Globe. "An agonizingly suspenseful thriller."—San Diego Tribune. "A grabber."—Seattle Times. "Timely, thought-provoking and definitely worth seeing."—San Diego Reader. "Entertaining, informative, thoughtful and scary."—The Weekly (Seattle). (#5056)

SHIVAREE
(LITTLE THEATRE—COMIC DRAMA)
By WILLIAM MASTROSIMONE
2 men, 3 women—Combination interior

We are delighted to publish this lesser-known but wonderful play by the acclaimed author of *Extremities* and *The Woolgatherer*. The story concerns a young hemophiliac youth named Chandler who has been kept, of necessity, by his cab driver mother in a very sheltered sort of existence. Chandler is desperate for contact with the world. He is also highly intelligent; but is supremely naive about the ways of the world. He pays a neighbor to bring him a girl; but he can't go through with his plans to have sex with her. He just doesn't know what to do about his craving for love—until he meets Shivaree. She is another neighbor who supports herself by being an itinerant belly-dancer. She is a True Original, and before too long the delightful Shivaree and the innocent Chandler are in love, much to the consternation of Chandler's mother, who forbids Chandler to ever see Shivaree again, throwing Shivaree out of Chandler's room. Chandler, undaunted, climbs out the fire escape—his first venture outside his hermetic world—going after his love. Fans of Mr. Mastrosimone's other plays will recognize the true-ness of the characterizations and the poignancy and humor of typical Mastrosimone dialogue in this wonderful play. (#21689)

Other Publications for Your Interest

COMING ATTRACTIONS
(ADVANCED GROUPS—COMEDY WITH MUSIC)

By TED TALLY, music by JACK FELDMAN, lyrics by BRUCE SUSSMAN and FELDMAN

5 men, 2 women—Unit Set

Lonnie Wayne Burke has the requisite viciousness to be a media celebrity—but he lacks vision. When we meet him, he is holding only four people hostage in a laundromat. There aren't any cops much less reporters around, because they're across town where some guy is holding 50 hostages. But, a talent agent named Manny sees possibilities in Lonnie Wayne. He devises a criminal persona for him by dressing him in a skeleton costume and sending him door-to-door, murdering people as "The Hallowe'en Killer". He is captured, and becomes an instant celebrity, performing on TV shows. When his fame starts to wane, he crashes the Miss America Pageant disguised as Miss Wyoming to kill Miss America on camera. However, he falls in love with her, and this eventually leads to his downfall. Lonnie ends up in the electric chair, and is fried "live" on prime-time TV as part of a jazzy production number! "Fizzles with pixilated laughter."—Time. "I don't often burst into gales of laughter in the theatre; here, I found myself rocking with guffaws."—New York Mag. "Vastly entertaining."—Newark Star-Ledger.

SORROWS OF STEPHEN
(ADVANCED GROUPS—COMEDY)

By PETER PARNELL

4 men, 5 women—Unit set

Stephen Hurt is a headstrong, impetuous young man—an irrepressible romantic—he's unable not to be in love. One of his models is Goethe's tragic hero, Werther, but as a contemporary New Yorker, he's adaptable. The end of an apparently undying love is followed by the birth of a grand new passion. And as he believes there's a literary precedent for all romantic possibilities justifying his choices—so with enthusiasm bordering on fickleness, he turns from Tolstoy, to Stendhal or Balzac. And Stephen's never discouraged—he can withstand rivers of rejection. (From the N.Y. Times.) And so his affairs—real and tentative—begin when his girl friend leaves him. He makes a romantic stab at a female cab driver, passes an assignation note to an unknown lady at the opera, flirts with an accessible waitress—and then has a tragic-with-comic-overtones, wild affair with his best friend's fiancée. "Breezy and buoyant. A real romantic comedy, sophisticated and sentimental, with an ageless attitude toward the power of positive love."—N.Y. Times.

Other Publications for Your Interest

PAST TENSE
(LITTLE THEATRE—DRAMA)

By JACK ZEMAN

1 man, 1 woman, 2 optional men—Interior

This compelling new play is about the breakup of a marriage. It is set on the day Emily and Ralphy Michaelson, a prosperous middle-aged couple, break off a union of 27 years. As they confront each other in their packed-up living room one final time, they alternately taunt and caress one another. She has never forgiven him for a petty infidelity of years ago. He has never forgiven her for her inability to express grief over the long-ago accidental death of their youngest child. In a series of flashbacks, Mr. Zeman dredges up the pivotal events of his characters' lives. Barbara Feldon and Laurence Luckinbill starred on Broadway in this at times humorous, and ultimately very moving play by a talented new playwright. " . . . rich in theatrical devices, sassy talk and promising themes."—N.Y. Times. "There is no doubt that Zeman can write. His backbiting, backlashing dialogue has considerable gusto—it belts out with a most impressively muscular vigor and intellectual vivacity."—N.Y. Post.

SCENES AND REVELATIONS
(ALL GROUPS—DRAMA)

By ELAN GARONZIK

3 men, 4 women—Platform set

Set in 1894 at the height of America's westward movement, the play portrays the lives of four Pennsylvania sisters who decide not to move west, but to England. It opens with the sisters prepared to leave their farm and birthplace forever. Then a series of lyrical flashbacks dramatize the tender and frustrating romances of the women. Rebecca, the youngest, marries and moves west to Nebraska, only to find she is ill-prepared for pioneer life. Millie, a bohemian artist, falls in love with the farm boy next door; when he marries a woman without Millie's worldly aspirations, she is crushed. Charlotte, a nurse, is rejected by her doctor on religious principles. Only Helena, the eldest, has the promise of a bright and bold life in California with Samuel, the farm's manager. However, Rebecca's tragic return east moves the sisters to unite for the promise of a better life in England. "A deeply human play . . . a rocket to the moon of imagination," Claudia Cassidy—WFMT, Chicago. "Humanly full . . . glimmers with revelation," Elliott—Chicago Sun-Times. "The play is a beauty," Sharp—WWD. "A deep understanding of women and their relationships with men," Barnes—New York Post.

Other Publications for Your Interest

THE CURATE SHAKESPEARE
AS YOU LIKE IT
(LITTLE THEATRE—COMEDY)

By DON NIGRO

4 men, 3 women—Bare stage

This extremely unusual and original piece is subtitled: ''The record of one company's attempt to perform the play by William Shakespeare''. When the very prolific Mr. Nigro was asked by a professional theatre company to adapt *As You Like It* so that it could be performed by a company of seven he, of course, came up with a completely original play about a rag-tag group of players comprised of only seven actors led by a dotty old curate who nonetheless must present Shakespeare's play; and the dramatic interest, as well as the comedy, is in their hilarious attempts to impersonate all of Shakespeare's multitude of characters. The play has had numerous productions nationwide, all of which have come about through word of mouth. We are very pleased to make this ''underground comic classic'' widely available to theatre groups who like their comedy wide open and theatrical.   (#5742)

SEASCAPE WITH SHARKS
AND DANCER
(LITTLE THEATRE—DRAMA)

By DON NIGRO

1 man, 1 woman—Interior

This is a fine new play by an author of great talent and promise. We are very glad to be introducing Mr. Nigro's work to a wide audience with *Seascape With Sharks and Dancer*, which comes directly from a sold-out, critically acclaimed production at the world-famous Oregon Shakespeare Festival. The play is set in a beach bungalow. The young man who lives there has pulled a lost young woman from the ocean. Soon, she finds herself trapped in his life and torn between her need to come to rest somewhere and her certainty that all human relationships turn eventually into nightmares. The struggle between his tolerant and gently ironic approach to life and her strategy of suspicion and attack becomes a kind of war about love and creation which neither can afford to lose. In other words, this is quite an offbeat, wonderful love story. We would like to point out that the play also contains a wealth of excellent **monologue** and **scene material.**   (#21060)

Other Publications for Your Interest

A WEEKEND NEAR MADISON
(LITTLE THEATRE—COMIC DRAMA)
By KATHLEEN TOLAN

2 men, 3 women—Interior

This recent hit from the famed Actors Theatre of Louisville, a terrific ensemble play about male-female relationships in the 80's, was praised by *Newsweek* as "warm, vital, glowing . . . full of wise ironies and unsentimental hopes". The story concerns a weekend reunion of old college friends now in their early thirties. The occasion is the visit of Vanessa, the queen bee of the group, who is now the leader of a lesbian/feminist rock band. Vanessa arrives at the home of an old friend who is now a psychiatrist hand in hand with her naif-like lover, who also plays in the band. Also on hand are the psychiatrist's wife, a novelist suffering from writer's block; and his brother, who was once Vanessa's lover and who still loves her. In the course of the weekend, Vanessa reveals that she and her lover desperately want to have a child—and she tries to persuade her former male lover to father it, not understanding that he might have some feelings about the whole thing. *Time Magazine* heard "the unmistakable cry of an infant hit . . . Playwright Tolan's work radiates promise and achievement." (#25051)

PASTORALE
(LITTLE THEATRE—COMEDY)
By DEBORAH EISENBERG

3 men, 4 women—Interior
(plus 1 or 2 bit parts and 3 optional extras)

"Deborah Eisenberg is one of the freshest and funniest voices in some seasons."—Newsweek. Somewhere out in the country Melanie has rented a house and in the living room she, her friend Rachel who came for a weekend but forgets to leave, and their school friend Steve (all in their mid-20s) spend nearly a year meandering through a mental landscape including such concerns as phobias, friendship, work, sex, slovenliness and epistemology. Other people happen by: Steve's young girlfriend Celia, the virtuous and annoying Edie, a man who Melanie has picked up in a bar, and a couple who appear during an intense conversation and observe the sofa is on fire. The lives of the three friends inevitably proceed and eventually draw them, the better prepared perhaps by their months on the sofa, in separate directions. "The most original, funniest new comic voice to be heard in New York theater since Beth Henley's 'Crimes of the Heart.'"—N.Y. Times. "A very funny, stylish comedy."—The New Yorker. "Wacky charm and wayward wit."—New York Magazine. "Delightful."—N.Y. Post. "Uproarious . . . the play is a world unto itself, and it spins."—N.Y. Sunday Times. (#18016)